Center for
Creative Leadership

leadership. learning. life.

Leading in Black and White

Working Across the Racial Divide in Corporate America

Ancella B. Livers
Keith A. Caver

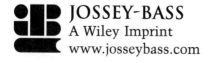
JOSSEY-BASS
A Wiley Imprint
www.josseybass.com

Center for
Creative Leadership
leadership. learning. life.

Published by Jossey-Bass
A Wiley Imprint
989 Market Street, San Francisco, CA 94103-1741   www.josseybass.com

Jossey-Bass books and products are available through most bookstores. To contact Jossey-Bass directly call our Customer Care Department within the U.S. at 800-956-7739, outside the U.S. at 317-572-3986 or fax 317-572-4002.

Jossey-Bass also publishes its books in a variety of electronic formats. Some content that appears in print may not be available in electronic books.

Library of Congress Cataloging-in-Publication Data
Livers, Ancella B., 1956-
  Leading in black and white : working across the racial divide in corporate America / by Ancella B. Livers and Keith A. Caver.
      p. cm.
Includes bibliographical references and index.
  ISBN 0-7879-5724-0 (acid-free)
  1. Afro-American executives. 2. Executives—United States. 3. Industrial management—United States. I. Caver, Keith A., 1957- II. Title.
  HD38.25.U6 L584 2003
  658.4'092'08996073—dc21   2002014352

Printed in the United States of America
FIRST EDITION
HB Printing 10 9 8 7 6 5 4 3 2 1

A joint publication in
The Jossey-Bass
Business & Management Series
and
The Center for Creative Leadership

To those who by their sacrifices and through whose vision
and determination these opportunities now exist.

Contents

Preface

Over the years, in working with more than a thousand African American professionals, we have heard innumerable tales of their workplace experiences. In listening to our colleagues' stories of everyday indignities, blatant racism, camaraderie, and special moments of good fortune, we have been struck by several things. First, we have noted how similar their tales are, regardless of the education, organization, job level, or geographical region of the storyteller. Second, we have realized how closely the stories mirrored our own work experiences. And third, we have been fascinated by the ways the experiences of black professionals differed from those of their non-black, mostly white, colleagues.

What we have seen time and again is that African American professionals today are well aware that they sit in positions that most of their grandparents could not fathom. They realize they have opportunities that many blacks today still have little chance of reaching. As one middle-aged manager puts it, "We are what they said we could not become." This statement sums up both the hope and the reality of the black corporate experience. That African Americans are in fact business leaders is the hope. That they have had to fight to achieve those positions, often at significant cost, is the reality. Everyone to whom we have spoken knows of many capable, qualified blacks who have been lost through the ignorance, bias, and just plain indifference of a system that could not see their worth and that could not see that as black managers they faced unique challenges. Some of these frustrated people have left the workplace; others stayed on, but their professional careers leveled off early.

We have also heard stories and witnessed situations that exemplify the confusion that many of the colleagues of black leaders experience in everyday interactions. "What did I do wrong?" they ask themselves after receiving a cool response to what they regarded as an innocuous comment. "What did we do wrong?" is the question that comes from the highest levels in the organization when a well-meant but misguided diversity effort intended to enhance opportunities for black managers or other nontraditional leaders has, once again, failed.

Every time we have heard another one of these stories or examples, we have shaken our heads and said, "What a waste," and then asked ourselves, "What can we do about it?" To answer the latter question, we set out, first, to document the problem: the lost opportunities, the missed communications, the distortions, the misunderstandings, the perceptual miscues, and hosts of other situations and behaviors. We drew on a strong Center for Creative Leadership legacy of research into diversity issues and practice in working with leaders on these issues, incorporating what we learned over the years from our work as co-facilitators of CCL's African-American Leadership Program; from CCL research on black-white relationships in the workplace, including the Lessons of a Diverse Workforce study; and from the work of Ann Morrison and CCL associates on diversity in the workplace, which resulted in the book *The New Leaders: Guidelines on Leadership Diversity in America*.

We also drew on the numerous other associations we have had with African American leaders, including working with and presenting to the National Black MBA Association, the National Association of Black Accountants, and the Congressional Black Caucus Foundation. From years of working with, thinking about, and observing and experiencing black work life, we began to understand some of the reasons for the differences between the leadership experience of black managers and that of their coworkers—particularly their white colleagues. We then used that information to show both African American leaders and those who work with them what they should know about the experience of being African American in the workplace. The result is the book you now hold in front of you.

Leading in Black and White tries to make much of what is invisible visible. It reports the experiences of the many professionals to whom we have talked, and some of these leaders speak directly to you through these pages. By illuminating the black experience in this way, we believe we can help people in the workplace understand one another better, and we can diminish the loss of professional dignity and enthusiasm experienced by many blacks. In this way we hope to help stem the incalculable loss of opportunity that afflicts talented black executives and to reduce the negative consequences for organizations.

August 2002   Ancella B. Livers
Greensboro, North Carolina   Keith A. Caver

Acknowledgments

First of all we want to extend our heartfelt appreciation to all the *leaders* who graciously let us observe them closely in their corporate settings. They freely shared their experiences, thoughts, and advice for bridging the gulf between what is and what can be. Whether in print, through face-to-face interviews, or over the telephone, their contributions provided the foundation for this book and fortified our vision of an enhanced corporate environment in which we all can be fully accepted and do our best work. Additionally, we want to thank all of our colleagues—both within the Center for Creative Leadership and otherwise, whose enthusiastic support enabled this effort to become a reality. These "cheerleaders" and enablers include our reviewers, endorsers, advisors, and confidants. The list of these special friends would be far too long to include here, but there are a few that require extra special recognition. Specifically, we want to thank Carl Bryant, Lily Kelly, Sara King, C. Howie Hodges, John Fleenor, Elizabeth Kersey, Mary White, and especially Stacey Ezell; and our editor, Marcia Horowitz—the dynamo whose energy and guidance have been a continual source of strength.

Ancella Acknowledges

I'd like to give my special thanks and love to my husband, Tony, and our sons, Lateef and Akil. Thank you for putting up with long days and weekends when the book seemed to take over everything. I know it wasn't easy, and I appreciate your support. I also want to thank my parents and cheerleaders, Nelson and Ancella Bickley, my in-laws, Claude and Florence Livers, and the rest of my family for their love and support throughout this project. You guys are great.

Keith Acknowledges

I've been blessed to have a chorus of supporters for everything I've ever done in life—they are simply known as family and include my wonderful parents, aunts and uncles, sisters and brothers, in-laws, and friends. Chief among them are my wife (and best friend), Cassandra, and our four beautiful children, Keith II, Bianca, Kendall, and Keenan (Alex). Their love, support, encouragement, and sterling examples of *servant leadership* have been the motivation and sustaining force for this effort.

The Authors

Ancella B. Livers is a manager of Individual Leader Development for the Center for Creative Leadership in Greensboro, North Carolina. In this role she manages and trains Foundations of Leadership and the Center's flagship offering, the Leadership Development Program (LDP)®. She also managed The African-American Leadership Program for five years, and currently trains in that program, and is past manager of The Women's Leadership Program. In addition to these responsibilities in the open-enrollment area, she designs and delivers custom programs to suit the specific needs of clients in the public, private, and nonprofit sectors. Livers is also a certified executive coach and feedback specialist. She was a member of the research team for CCL's Lessons of a Diverse Workforce, a multiyear study of 288 diverse managers. The study's primary function was to explore the significant events from which African Americans learn and develop and whether these events are different from those typical of whites.

Prior to joining CCL, Livers was assistant professor in the School of Journalism at West Virginia University. Earlier in her career she served as acting business editor and Capitol Hill reporter for the Gannett News Service and appeared as a regular guest on the Baltimore public affairs television show *Urban Scene*. Livers holds an M.S. degree in journalism from Northwestern University and M.A. and Ph.D. degrees in history from Carnegie Mellon University. She has published several articles and a book chapter on the role of race in the workplace and has presented and facilitated widely at such venues as the Fortune 500 Conference and In Council with Women in Cleveland.

Keith A. Caver is director of the Client and Assessment Services Group at the Center for Creative Leadership in Greensboro, North Carolina. In this role he is responsible for all client management activities and for CCL testing and assessment services. He also serves as a senior program associate, designing and training client-specific programs. Caver is a core trainer for both the Leadership Development Program (LDP)® and The African-American Leadership Program. He has facilitated seminars on an array of leadership subjects ranging from change management to diversity, at such organizations as Verizon, Duke University, General Motors, and The Chubb Corporation and was a member of CCL's Lessons of a Diverse Workforce research team.

Prior to joining CCL, Caver spent twenty years as an officer in the U.S. Air Force, where he engaged in operations management, quality control, and diplomatic service and acquired extensive leadership experience in varied roles in the United States and abroad. Additionally, he taught management courses at the University of Maryland at College Park (European Division) and was an assistant professor at North Carolina Agricultural and Technical State University in Greensboro. Caver holds a B.S. degree in management from Park University and an M.S. degree in management from the Air Force Institute of Technology. He has completed postgraduate studies through the University of Alabama and is a graduate of the University of North Carolina, Chapel Hill, Senior Executive Program. Caver is a certified executive coach and feedback specialist, authorized to administer a variety of assessments and evaluations.

Introduction

Kevin's comment hung in the air for less than five seconds, but for the group it seemed like hours. Half an hour earlier, twelve executives had entered the classroom as complete strangers. There were several stiff smiles, a few broad ones, and a nod or two of general acknowledgment. Kevin was the first to go through the formal introduction process. As instructed by the program facilitators, he talked from a drawing he had made depicting his introductory information: his name, what he did, something of which he was proud, and something about him that was not on his résumé. He responded to the last prompt with a drawing of a cookie. "This may be a bit controversial," he said, "but this is a cookie, and you'll notice that it has only one chip in it. That's me. I'm usually the only chocolate chip in the cookie. You can make of that what you want." Then Kevin, the only African American among the participants, smiled, hung his picture on the wall, and sat down. Those awkward seconds passed, then another participant stood up to continue the introduction process.

Days later a portion of the same group met again in preparation for giving feedback to Kevin. This particular session included three white men, all of whom were still bothered by Kevin's introductory comments. "He played the race card," said one. "He made me feel as if I were attacked," said another. "Later, when I got to know him, he was a great guy," said the third, "but it made it harder for me to get to know him at first. I just thought he came here to learn like I did, and then I realized he was really angry about some workplace issues."

Kevin said he expected the response he received but that his introduction was his way of pushing people to acknowledge that he was black. As a man who had been educated at a largely white, exclusive university and who worked in a predominantly white corporation, he felt it was important that his colleagues consciously recognize that his work and leadership experiences were different from theirs and that this difference was important. Kevin, who routinely introduced himself in the fashion described here, explained that he wasn't trying to make his white colleagues feel guilty or uncomfortable. Rather, the point he was making was larger than himself—he was doing this to try to help other African Americans. He wanted whites to understand that what they call a "color-blind workforce" is not color-blind at all, that people's unwillingness to understand what it means to be the "only chocolate chip in the cookie" makes his and other African Americans' jobs more difficult.

It took a great deal of further discussion and follow-up before Kevin's colleagues understood his point. For them, Kevin had thrown down the gauntlet—a challenge made even more perplexing by his subsequently friendly behavior. Why had such a nice guy introduced himself in such an inflammatory way? they asked. Why had he brought up race when they had not even noticed it?

Such differences in perspective and the ways these differences affected the interactions between Kevin and his colleagues are at the heart of this book. Kevin felt it was important to acknowledge his blackness, but despite his benign intentions, his actions prompted his colleagues to feel defensive and react negatively. Kevin's colleagues felt that race should be irrelevant or ignored among professionals and were disturbed because they now felt forced to deal with it. However, Kevin's experience had taught him that the issue of race was inextricably woven into his workplace interactions and opportunities and that having his colleagues come to understand this experience and its lessons would be vital to the success of their working together. What made this a miscommunication initially were Kevin's and his colleagues' different understandings of the role race plays in the workplace. It is this miscommunication and its impact, directly at the nexus of race and leadership, that we seek to address in Leading in Black and White. The desire of so many is to view leadership as color-blind when the reality is far more nuanced. At the same time, we look at the impact on productivity of the unique leadership challenges faced by African Americans and at the many practical steps people of all races can take to improve communication and understand the serious implications for everyone of failing to breach the racial divide. No, this is not the same old conversation about race but rather a brand new one, one that goes to a new level of understanding about what it is like to be black in a predominantly white workplace, one that also aims to peel away the layers of misunderstanding and confusion.

The Dynamics of a Changing Workplace

Look around you. The demographics of the workplace have changed, and right in the center of this change is the increase in numbers of male and female black leaders. For several years now they have become more visible at all levels of corporate America. Their path has been eased by the legal and workplace remedies instituted in the last thirty years. Black managers now fill all roles in the workplace: they are visible at the highest levels of leadership, in middle management, and as young professionals beginning their careers. Blacks represent multinational companies in all corners of the world. A good number of people report to black managers, and a good number of people manage them.

As a result of this increasing diversity, the level of interaction between black managers and their colleagues has increased considerably, and the character of these interactions has changed. Where there was once a hierarchy that allocated power in the workplace to senior white males, the distribution of power has now become more diffuse. Increasingly, minorities and women are in senior-level positions in which they wield considerable influence. And according to the latest census data, these numbers are on the rise. The 1990 census reported that 13.2 percent of black men and 19.5 percent of black women were employed in managerial or professional roles. By the 2000 census, these numbers had risen to 17.7 percent and 25.2 percent, respectively.

This changing environment inevitably results in more situations where power differentials and race mix in new ways, producing interactions that can be misunderstood by either or both parties—and that consequently may be laden with friction. For white professionals such situations can be frustrating. But for black managers these misunderstandings can lead to profound disappointment in a personal and collective dream. For them these misunderstandings can also have significant professional ramifications. From one or two difficult interactions, a reputation, a legacy, or a series of misperceptions may accrue, leading to diminished performance. These consequences often isolate or estrange black leaders from the mainstream and, worst of all, may deny them opportunities that appear within reach but are in truth disappointingly remote.

The reality is that many blacks in the workplace face a set of dynamics unique to those who are nontraditional—and, specifically, African American—in a traditionally white male-dominated world. These dynamics influence and affect their communication with whites, other blacks, and other people of color. They result in greater personal pressures and workplace challenges. And they can affect access to professional opportunities. When faced with poor encounters or working relationships, blacks are left to consider whether race or personality is a factor. They are often confused about what part of a failed interaction they should take personal responsibility for, what part has to do with others' assumptions and expectations, and what part is simply "the way things work." All of these extra burdens and potentially negative consequences lead to a state of unease in black managers that we call *miasma*.

People who work with African American leaders encounter the flip side of these invisible dynamics of race. They may assume that the workplace is a level playing field and be unaware of the nuances of the very different African American corporate experience. They may, however, be aware of awkwardness or feel unsure in their interactions with black professionals. Some may also realize that this confusion inhibits the communication needed for effective performance and that it can lead to strained relationships between the people involved. At a basic level this discomfort or tension has ramifications for individual working relationships. In addition it can inhibit a team or group, along with virtually anyone else who has a stake in the work.

On a systemic level, many organizations that employ African Americans are confounded by what they delicately refer to as "the problem." Why are their diversity programs ineffective? Why are they losing valuable African American employees? Why is it that no matter what they try it isn't enough or it isn't effective? How can they spend time building potential in their black management population, instead of trying to undo the damage of failed interactions? Faced with an increasingly diverse workforce and an increasingly global marketplace, organizations that are successfully tapping into the diversity of their workforce will gain in organizational knowledge and insight. By taking advantage of individuals' diverse contributions, they can benefit from flexible and highly effective leadership.

Leading in Black and White aims to cut through the miasma for black leaders *and* the confusion of those who work with them. It aims to further everyone's understanding of difference and to provide a practical framework for more productive communications and interactions.

Traditional and Nontraditional Leadership

Through our research, our observations, and our experiences we have found that there are six significant areas in which black leaders interpret the workplace and interact in that workplace differently. At the everyday level of give-and-take, much of what happens when there are failures in communication and perception is often a result of differing perspectives of black leaders by others who work and interact with them. These differing perspectives are in some way related to black leaders' distinctive approaches to identity, feelings of responsibility for other blacks, heightened attention to race and gender, challenges in networking, need for mentoring, and approaches to office politics. Identifying these six areas of difference, however, is just the first step. Understanding them and especially what can be done about them is where the real work lies.

We emphasize that whether something is true or is just perceived to be true is not the issue when it comes to the impact on individuals' experience. If something is perceived, it is believed, and as such it will affect actions and responses. By focusing on perceptions and working to understand them, leaders and their organizations can correct the *mis*perceptions about race that plague the corporate sector and prevent new ones from gaining a foothold.

We also emphasize that although more cross-race interactions can mean more potential for failure, they can also mean more potential for increased understanding that leads to success for individuals and for organizations. Failed interactions of any kind— whether resulting from simple misunderstandings or full-blown altercations—are the responsibilities of all parties involved. Although it is difficult to address communication failures in the context of power differentials (which often are truly or are perceived to be present in a racial context), that is the challenge of and ultimately the motivation for writing this book: to expose the assumptions that lead to miscommunication and to provide information and recommendations that can help all leaders improve communication and workplace relationships.

Where We Got Our Ideas

The thinking that underlies this book and the approach we have chosen represent a culmination of extensive personal and professional research. As faculty at the Center for Creative Leadership, we listened time and again as African American professionals described experiences that paralleled each other's—and our own. In pursuit of the *whys* behind this commonality, we drew upon 39 in-depth interviews of African Americans conducted by CCL from 1996 to 1997. Between 1999 and 2000, we surveyed approximately 270 African American professionals and, between 2000 and 2001, personally interviewed another 20 black professionals in depth. The resulting data, including the conversations and impressions we gathered from regularly training corporate leaders, both black and white, are the basis for the content and the conclusions of this work. As you will see, we present many of the interviewees' own words throughout the book. We've used pseudonyms and altered job titles to protect the interviewees' confidentiality and to underscore the point that their experiences, although individual, may also be universal.

Most existing publications about African Americans' experiences in organizations describe the effects of discriminatory workplaces or the career paths of highly successful African American businesspeople. The ideas in this book go to another level of understanding of black workplace experience. *Leading in Black and White* offers a close examination of the assumptions that guide corporate and individual attitudes toward black managers, including some of the attitudes that black managers hold themselves. Rather than focus on the difficulties that attend African Americans' entry into management, this book enters the world of the work experience itself, looking closely at the sociopolitical environment that influences the performance and mind-sets of black managers. The rich texture of the stories and feelings that permeate the text comes from black professionals' perspectives on and interpretations of their working environments.

Who Should Read This Book and How Best to Use It

When people say something concerns "race," whites and also some people of color tend to think, "Oh, it's for Them." But racial issues are issues about and between *all* races, not just people of color. They are not about "us" or "them" but about how we all relate with one another. Although it is ambitious to write for multiple audiences, we firmly believe that a shortcoming in diversity literature is that it tends to focus on one group or the other, usually spotlighting the "problem" group. Yet the issues that face African Americans and other nontraditional leaders do not belong to only one group or to a conglomerate of "problem" people. Instead, they are matters that involve all who work in corporations and other organizations in America. Thus this book is aimed at a broad audience as it explores ways through and around the complexities of creating a diverse workforce.

We believe that the only way to change issues of race is for all parties to understand them and work toward improvement. So the primary audience for this work is both black corporate leaders *and* those who work with them. The discussions and strategies are intended for executives, managers, peers, direct reports, young professionals, and human resource professionals of all colors. We believe that *Leading in Black and White* will give people in the workplace a better understanding of how blacks may experience leadership differently from whites and how that difference affects both how blacks lead and how they are perceived by others at work. Most chapters conclude with practical applications for black professionals and for those that work with them. Readers who are not black but who are nontraditional may find that many of these applications resonate for them as well.

For black leaders, it is our hope that this work will help them to understand and articulate the factors in their work world that cause stress and those that create support. Most of the chapters offer black leaders strategies on how to negotiate the workplace and also challenge them to consider how they might think and behave differently to increase their effectiveness. Each leader can use these strategies to determine his or her own best course of action and then engage the resources needed to act on that course. Further, with this work we hope to assure African Americans that they are not alone in their work experiences, that the data and the stories of countless professionals support their interpretation of events.

For those who work with black leaders, it is our hope that this book will illuminate African Americans' perceptions and experiences of the workplace, making the invisible visible. Beyond describing the differences, moreover, this book attempts to explain why they exist. Most chapters offer specific strategies for non-black readers on how they might work more successfully with blacks, and this book challenges them to consider how they might think and behave differently to increase their own effectiveness. Not intended to point fingers or to lay blame, this book encourages individuals to put defensiveness aside, examine their personal assumptions and responsibilities, and consider the role each person has in workplace interactions.

Non-black readers who are nontraditional in other ways may find both validation and insights in the experiences of African American professionals. Although specific experiences may differ, the dynamics may be similar. This book provides an opportunity for these readers to reflect on their experiences, the overall dynamics of the corporate workplace, and how they themselves play into or against the traditional norms. As a result the strategy sections for African Americans and those for their colleagues may be useful to these readers. The work in this book can and should be generalized to other nontraditional groups, such as Latinos and women and people with disabilities. Indeed, we believe that focusing on one group and understanding some of the issues that face that group is a way to begin understanding how to determine the issues other groups face. Through such investigations all who work in organizations may begin to comprehend more about the contexts in which these groups are being asked to lead.

How This Book Is Organized

Part One of this book (Chapters One through Seven) explores the issues that combine to assist and hinder black professionals as they go about their work lives. Chapter One offers a general description of black corporate life and its effect on black managers, drawing a dramatic picture of the condition we call miasma and its influence on everyday work. Then each of the six remaining chapters in Part One looks at one of the six areas of difference for black professionals (perceptions of identity, feelings of responsibility for other blacks, heightened attention to race and gender, challenges in networking, need for mentoring, and approaches to office politics). Each chapter begins with an illustration of the difference in action and then goes on to describe what the difference looks like from the perspective of the black leader, in what way it is unique to the black experience, and how it plays out in the workplace. Chapters Two through Seven go back to the debilitating impact of miasma again and again and show how each difference factor both drives and reacts to it. Most important are the concluding sections of each chapter, containing specific recommendations for black managers and for their colleagues on how to think and act in ways that lead to productive interactions. Interestingly, in some cases the recommendations are the same for both blacks and non-blacks.

Reading the chapters in Part One in sequence is important because the discussion of each area of difference draws on or is affected by the previous areas.

The discussion of identity, in Chapter Two, explores the foundation for the difference black leaders experience in corporate America. For most of the African Americans we surveyed, being black is one of the most salient issues in their workplace experience. Although it grants them a sense of uniqueness, often it is also accompanied by a sense of loss.

Following the discussion of identity is an examination of taking responsibility for others, in Chapter Three. The idea of looking after other blacks is a self-imposed notion that stems partially from the group identity and environmentally induced identity crisis that many blacks share. Helping each other is black professionals' way of compensating for an environment that may not be willing to help them.

A look at the impact of perceptions about race and gender comes next, in Chapter Four, because many African Americans grant primary allegiance to race and the responsibilities that flow from this identity. However, even with a full understanding of their racial identity, some leaders recognize that race and gender combine to create a different set of dynamics than either race or gender alone imposes. This chapter also discusses the different experiences of black men and black women.

The examination of using networking strategies, in Chapter Five, tackles the broad-based skills associated with working through others. Networking can help blacks reverse some of the fragmentation created by the loss of identity, the burden of responsibility, and the challenges associated with race and gender issues. The process of networking, however, can also pose special challenges for African American professionals.

Mentoring, discussed in Chapter Six, is in many ways a refinement of the networking concept. Through mentoring, leaders use honed networking skills to partner with others for purposeful professional growth and development. Because mentoring opportunities are scarce for blacks, they may also be implicitly challenged to expand their views about mentoring relationships and about assuming mentoring responsibilities themselves.

The idea of being politically savvy, addressed in Chapter Seven, serves to integrate the preceding issues by providing insights into ways of navigating all the previous issues and discussing ways of maximizing personal strengths and opportunities to increase African American leaders' effectiveness in corporate America.

Part Two (Chapters Eight through Ten) helps readers evaluate overall actions they can take to address the six areas of difference described in Part One. Chapter Eight is directed at African American leaders and suggests steps they can take to improve their work experience. Chapter Nine is addressed to white and other colleagues of black leaders, providing guidelines for alternate ways to think about situations and interactions and for approaching interactions with African Americans differently. Chapter Ten is a broader look at the steps organizations, as entities directed by senior executives, can take to acknowledge differences in leadership experiences, to facilitate greater understanding of diversity, and to encourage more effective interpersonal interactions.

An Appendix offers an assessment tool that leaders may use to gain some insights into themselves and their work environments. The list of references includes additional books on the subject that may be consulted for further reading.

PART ONE

A World of Difference for Black Managers

1

The Assumption of Similarity

As we explain in the Introduction, there are six major areas in which black managers may perceive and experience the workplace differently from their mostly white colleagues. But before we get into these areas of difference that are the heart of this book, let's talk a bit about the ways two omnipresent factors in the lives of black managers—the assumption of similarity and the effect of miasma—influence how and why black managers take a different approach to the workplace.

The Assumption of Similarity

The subject line of the e-mail says simply, "Working While Black." If you're an African American leader in corporate America, you've probably had this popular message forwarded to you. Its one-liners pointedly describe the black corporate experience.

- A coworker sees you and several black colleagues at a casual lunch. Back at the office she asks, "What was the meeting all about?"
- You tell your manager about a problem you are having and the response you get is, "You have got to be exaggerating! I find that hard to believe."

- You are told you are "rough around the edges" despite your completion of many professional development programs, and it is suggested you emulate the behavior of a person not of color.

- You are being recognized at a company banquet. As you approach the stage to receive your company's highest achievement award, your corporation's top executive exclaims, "Yo, homeboy, congratulations."

- After a coworker returns from a weekend in the sun, he runs to you on Monday morning and extending his arms to touch yours says, "Hey, I'm darker than you."

- You continually get more responsibility, but no authority.

- You have to perform at 250% to stay even.

- You have to document everything. You've learned the hard way.

The comments that have accompanied this e-mail—such as "Can I get a witness?" and "Amen!"—indicate that African Americans are having similar experiences in the workplace—and they aren't always pleasant. Regularly, often daily, African Americans are reminded through jokes, seemingly innocent statements, job assignments, and work relationships that they are different and, more important, that the difference is not a good one.

The irony is that the workplace often does not acknowledge these experiences. Although most workplaces do not tolerate blatant discrimination, the subtle signs suggest they remain inhospitable to blacks and other nontraditional leaders. By upholding an assumption that all people experience an equitable workplace—an *assumption of similarity* where there is a reality of difference—corporations create a fiction that many people accept as truth. This supposed truth, however, is one-sided because it takes into account only one perspective. As Lena Williams says in her book *It's the Little Things*, "Another ordinary thing that riles many of us and fuels mistrust between the races is the assumption that we blacks are supposed to accept white people's word as the truth, the whole truth, and nothing but the truth, when our basic instincts tell us otherwise." It may be that the corporate workplace holds up this fiction of equality because it believes, misguidedly, that being "color-blind" will result in equal opportunity. It may also be that the workplace does not even consider the issue of color, whether to acknowledge it or deny it.

Instead of leveling the playing field, this assumption of similarity where there is a reality of difference serves to marginalize blacks and other nontraditional leaders. By turning a blind eye to the ways in which people of color experience unique, additional challenges in the workplace, this approach places blacks on unequal footing. For example, the assumption of similarity allows people to question the credibility of anyone who suggests that equal treatment is not taking place. By assuming that the playing field is level, non-black colleagues are able to dismiss charges of subtle discrimination. Write Joe R. Feagin and Melvin P. Sikes, in *Living with Racism: The Black Middle Class Experience*, "One more aspect of the burden of being black is having to defend one's understanding of events to white acquaintances without being labeled as racially paranoid."

Minimizing the diverse experiences of people of color can lead to minimizing their contributions as well. People of color bring a different data set to certain corporate conversations because they have had different experiences both in and out of work. However, if corporate leaders don't recognize or value those experiences, they are unlikely to tap into the knowledge and insight to be gained from them. As a result their corporations as well as the individuals involved suffer.

The Effect of Miasma

Imagine going to work each day with the anticipation of running up against misperceptions, distortions, and sometimes completely fictional accounts of your behaviors from colleagues. "Maybe it will happen today and maybe it won't," the black manager might muse, for the possibility of misunderstanding is always lurking. This murky atmosphere of misperception and distortion in which black managers must work is a condition we call *miasma*. In simple terms, it operates like a low-lying cloud, surrounding those who have to bear extra burdens and exert extra energy in ways that are not directly related to the work itself. Black leaders respond to it with a certain wariness, a perceived self-defensive stance, and an expenditure of time and energy that is counterproductive or at the very least stifling.

The inverse relationship of miasma and the degree to which there is an acceptance of difference in organizations is shown in Figure 1.1.When nontraditional leaders work with others or in organizations that have a low tolerance for individual or cultural difference, the resulting miasma they operate within becomes denser and potentially more difficult in which to maneuver. Increased miasma can lead to degraded communication, interpersonal interactions, and work performance as individuals become increasingly guarded, uncomfortable, and less participatory in their organizations. Conversely, in those organizations with a higher degree of acceptance for the difference of others, the miasma is less dense and more easily managed. In these instances, nontraditional leaders benefit from enhanced recognition, understanding, and valuing of their unique perspectives and potential contributions.

FIGURE 1.1. The Difference Factor.

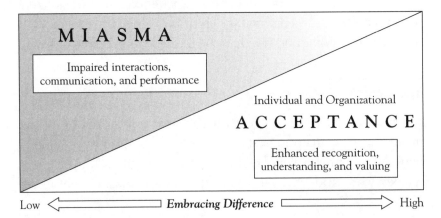

MIASMA

Impaired interactions, communication, and performance

Individual and Organizational
ACCEPTANCE

Enhanced recognition, understanding, and valuing

Low ⟵ *Embracing Difference* ⟶ High

For African American managers, miasma gets more dense every time they experience communications that may be laden with preconceptions, misconceptions, or lack of understanding. For example, a black leader might find herself in a situation where she thinks, "I'm being proactive, but he thinks I'm being aggressive." Black leaders in such cases experience a host of emotions, second-guess their reactions, and are fundamentally paralyzed when they could be moving forward. It is a drain on the individual and ultimately a drain on the organization.

Miasma is diaphanous, like a fog, difficult to grasp but ever present. The miasma surrounding any one person can be more or less dense depending on the individual situation and the people involved. Miasma is created by the introduction of difference into a situation and the responses to that difference. This action and reaction takes benign elements of difference, identity for example, and makes them flashpoints—areas that are rife for misinterpretation and misunderstanding. These elements and the cloud they create are miasma. The salient points of difference will vary for each nontraditional group, but the impact they have on the groups can be similar. If left unacknowledged and unmanaged, miasma can make individual and organizational relationships between nontraditional leaders and their more traditional counterparts more difficult and it can lessen organizational effectiveness. In our research on miasma, we found the six areas that are most salient for African Americans are identity, responsibility, race and gender, networking, mentoring, and being politically savvy (see Figure 1.2).

An important goal for black managers is to discover how to work through miasma and not be impeded by it. The goal for organizations and for non-black colleagues who work within these organizations should be twofold: to understand the dynamic miasma creates for black leaders, and to determine how to reduce miasma to ensure that the organization is poised to best support and benefit from the efforts of all workers.

The effect of miasma is easier to see than the thing itself. In both our research at the Center for Creative Leadership and our

FIGURE 1.2. The Miasma of Black Leaders.

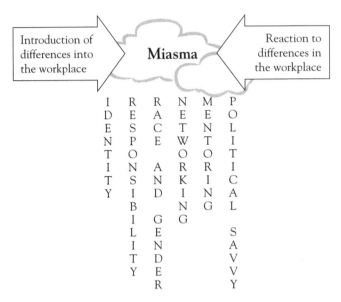

personal experiences, we have found that miasma has three major effects on African Americans:

- It reduces their trust in others.
- It fosters the belief that they must work twice as hard as others.
- It means that they can never let down their guard.

These beliefs are unique and omnipresent burdens that many blacks carry. They create additional stress for black leaders working in traditionally white male workplaces. To navigate these real and perceived challenges requires the expenditure of an enormous amount of energy not usually required of whites.

Anna Dutch, senior executive for a professional sports team, compares her work experience to that of her white colleagues. First, Anna says, it took her a long time to feel she had the skills and confidence to compete with others. Beyond that, her road to success was far more challenging. As she explains with a vivid metaphor, although they were all "headed in the same direction," her colleagues could make the journey in a brand-new sports utility vehicle, while she had to drive an old, battered wreck. "My tires are all messed up and the gas tank is not as large. When they jump out of the car at the top of the hill, they're all refreshed. I jump out and I'm all worn out. I'm excited for being there, but I wonder if it's worth it."

It's a Matter of Trust

As we listened to professional after professional tell stories of their day-to-day journey to leadership, the issue of trust prevailed as a theme in their similar experiences, regardless of the original topic of discussion. Being able to trust others is the linchpin for successful professional relationships, but trust can be risky for African American leaders, both on the individual and organizational front.

For African Americans the issue of trust in personal and professional relationships is especially important. The history of slavery and discrimination has bred distrust of the system, because trust has been so often broken. Bill Wilton, an associate manager at an insurance company, says that if he were giving advice to incoming African Americans he would tell them, "Don't trust anybody until you know they can be trusted. There's a lot of people who will walk up to you and be friendly and stuff, but they're trying to pull information out of you so they can use it against you." Although this may sound extreme, it reflects the sentiments of many people we have interviewed.

"I'm finding that I don't trust my peers that often," says Sam Masters, an employee services manager. "I'm very leery of them." Moreover, he believes his peers don't trust him either. In talking with Sam it is clear that his problem with trust is not a concern about individual integrity but a concern about communication between people who are simply uncomfortable with each other because they are of different races. Critical but often elusive, trust is fragile—and it can so easily be sundered.

James Kelley, a sales specialist for a health-care products organization, agrees with Bill Wilton. In general James does not trust his work colleagues, and this sometimes influences the interactions he has or the decisions he makes. "Typically," he says, "I'm more likely to make safe decisions than chancy ones." Although he recognizes that well-considered risks might be better for the organization overall and even for his career, James's inability to trust leaves him playing it safe. "I don't think I can trust my boss," he said.

Tyrone Billington, general manager for a utility company, speaks for many as he points out that trust is based in similarity of experience and perspective. "The only people I can truly trust are African Americans, and we're in such limited numbers. I can trust white colleagues only up to a point. I can't afford to open myself up to somebody who doesn't have my experience." Keith Shields, senior vice president of a financial institution, has a slightly different perspective. Says Shields, "I trust everyone—up to 80 percent—regardless of their race," indicating that for some black executives, the granting of trust is a significant privilege, one to be selectively bestowed on others.

Working Twice as Hard

In addition to believing that they must be cautious with their trust, many African American leaders believe they must work twice as hard as their coworkers to achieve the same results. This issue comes up routinely in CCL's African-American Leadership Program. In their book *Soul in Management*, Richard F. America and Bernard E. Anderson dispute the accuracy of this belief but acknowledge its pervasiveness in the black community. It comes up, they say, "in workshops, conferences, books and casual conversation." This belief is also prevalent in the black professional community. And although there are no data to support this contention, that does not invalidate African Americans' concern. Part of the problem is that the issue has not been directly studied. However, the data represented in this book, including data from many of the studies we cite and the results from the numerous interviews we conducted, indicate that there may be more truth to this perception than previously documented.

In addition to voicing his concerns about issues of trust, Sam Masters says, "[I feel] like I constantly have to prove myself." James Washington, a manager at a national chemical company, echoes this belief. In order to be successful, he feels he has to have record earnings. "I have to have strategies that . . . have a hell of a lot more impact and so forth," he says. "I just have to do that."

Nan Blunt, a manager for an executive development firm, explains that ever since her high school integrated she has believed she has to demonstrably prove her worth. Her adult experiences have underscored this notion, leading Blunt to always overprepare for professional tasks. "I'm clear it's a race thing," she says. "I'm going to prove I'm competent." Although Blunt admits that racial considerations have not stopped the upward mobility of her career, she believes her practice of working twice as hard has a lot to do with her success. Despite that success, though, the extra work is tiring and stressful. But because she refuses to give people an excuse to question her abilities, Blunt states, "I always will work harder."

When he worked at a national manufacturer of household goods, Dan Carole recognized how and why he had to work harder than his colleagues. As the first African American account manager, he says, "I wanted to pave the way for others."

Keeping Your Guard Up

The notion that African Americans, through their behaviors, are responsible for the opportunities that will be given to other African Americans is another pervasive belief in the black professional community. In our survey, 51 percent of African American business professionals said they believed that if they made a mistake at work other blacks would be adversely affected. In the same survey, 95 percent of black professionals said they felt responsible for helping other African Americans succeed in their organizations. As a result, many black professionals almost always feel they have to keep their guard up. Just being at work means having to watch and beware.

A corporate training consultant explains why keeping your guard up is necessary: it is a self-protective stance that ensures you always remain poised and prepared. Being African American in a traditional workplace requires continual defense, he says, similar to the diligence and deft maneuvering of a boxer. "I always have to keep that right arm up. If I drop it, if I tire, I show weakness. I become vulnerable to jabs, blows, and the occasional roundhouse—all of which I'm used to deflecting but any of which, if they were to get through, could be a blow from which I can't recover." Although the effort required to keep one's guard up can take a toll, the potential cost of letting it down is far greater.

Nan Blunt has thought about the challenge of keeping her guard up without being overwhelmed by the energy that takes. "People don't see me as always having my battle gear on, but internally these things challenge me. I have to be more personally 'on.' . . . I may need to keep my battle clothes on, but I also need to be clear which is my battle and which is not my battle. All battles are not mine to fight. All things are not equal, but maybe I'm not in a war all the time. War is not about things people see. Maybe it's what I'm doing myself in the course of doing battle. I'm carrying all my gear. I'm tired."

Adding It All Up

Many of the African Americans we interviewed or surveyed have discussed the burden and stress they feel because they are black in corporate America. At each step, whether it is trust, responsibility, or feeling as if they have to work twice as hard, they explained the pressure these concerns add to their work life. "You constantly have to be conscious about things that other people don't have to worry about," said Rita Farax, an HR director at a national chemical company. "It's just so much pressure," says Anna Dutch. She recalls the time when a white man in her office made a costly mistake. In discussing the incident he said, "If I don't make a mistake every day, it means I'm not trying." "I was floored," says Dutch, "because if I make a mistake every day, I'm fired. I thought, they can make a mistake. I could not believe it."

For African Americans the effects of this workplace stress are not additive but multiplicative. Black managers say they don't feel just a little more stress, they feel encompassed by it. "The stress associated with race can have a pervasive effect on all aspects of your life," says Darlene Winchester, a bank diversity manager.

The lesson that many blacks learn from work and other social experiences is that race always matters and it always matters all of the time. "In a very general way," says Deborah Raleigh, vice president of a national retail and food manufacturer, "it means that as a minority in a majority group, I will be different. Everything I do will be different. Even if I do the same things that everybody else does, it will be viewed as different because I'm different. And so I either live with that or get over it in order to survive."

Because they believe they are being treated and seen differently from many of their coworkers, black managers chafe against the rhetoric that denies their experience and tells them that all is equal. Consequently, when asked what their organizations could do differently, many African American leaders said they want their companies to see them as human beings, full partners in an organization in which they too have a vested interest. Their wish, like those of many who are disenfranchised in the workplace, is that the corporate assumption of similarity would evolve to one of acceptance and the valuing of difference for everyone.

We have looked briefly at two challenges that black managers face daily—the assumption of similarity and the effect of miasma—with the goal of laying a broad foundation for understanding the experience of black managers in the workplace. In Chapters Two through Seven, we explore in depth the six primary areas in which black managers perceive and respond to the workplace differently from their non-black colleagues. In Chapter Two you will see how context and miasma affect the fundamental issue of one's identity, both in and out of the workplace. As we uncover what African American leaders are saying about their experiences, we will suggest practical strategies for what they and others can do to create more positive outcomes.

2

Who Are We?

For years Marcella Watkins had worn a wig. Her mother had made her wear a wig since she was a child, to protect her from others who taunted her about her short hair. Girls, especially black girls, were expected to have long hair. If girls had short hair, it was assumed their hair wouldn't grow and that they were less attractive, less feminine than those with long, or "good," hair. When she was in college, Marcella quit wearing the hated wig and felt free for the first time; it was like removing a mask or, better yet, laying down a heavy burden. But when Marcella got a job following school, she reluctantly donned the wig again. When Marcella considered working without the wig, Marcella's mother told her it might come down to her hair or her job.

So Marcella continued to wear the wig, feeling more diminished each day because she feared she wouldn't be accepted. The wig became a symbol that she could not be accepted as she was—not at work, not at home. After much struggle, Marcella realized that when wearing the wig she felt empty and lost but that if she were to give up the wig she could maintain her sense of self. Even if it meant losing her job, as long as she maintained her sense of self, she thought she could probably manage. So she stopped wearing the wig—false impression be damned! And to her surprise and relief, she was not fired.

As Marcella, now a director in a major accounting firm, tells this story her voice is soft yet rich with emotion. For years now she has worn her hair short, but the pain of not being accepted for what she was and the fear of losing her job because of a hairstyle have marked her. Coming through this experience has made Marcella resolute about matters of identity. She will be who she is, what she is, wherever she is, of that she is now sure. If there is a price for maintaining her sense of self, she is willing to pay it. Having had to fight for her identity, she is loathe to give it up ever again.

Marcella's intense feelings about identity, like those of many African Americans, stem from having had others attempt to define what her identity should be. Questions of identity swirl around African Americans in the workplace like ghosts: What is "too black" for white standards? What is "black enough" for African American standards? How is color perceived in supposedly color-blind settings? Like ghosts, identity issues can be fearful, haunting the workplace and causing people to be overlooked in their jobs, to lose their jobs, and in extreme instances to lose themselves.

What Identity Looks Like

There are many ways to define identity, each illuminating a part of something that is profoundly important yet difficult to pin down with words. Identity is a dynamic interaction between *how others perceive us* and *how we conceive of ourselves*. It is influenced by many factors, such as race, gender, generational age, economic class, education, geographical location, and personal and collective history. Our identity may be revealed to others through the visible expressions of our beliefs that associate us with a larger group of people. These expressions of belief include things like our language and attire, how we relate experiences, and the actions that reflect our connection to the larger group. Although identity can be embodied in our physical and verbal expressions, it is important to remember that it is more than that. We also express identity in our individual actions; we honor our identity with self-confidence and pride.

Part of our identity involves our reciprocal relationship with our larger collective—we receive from this group and at the same time feel responsibility toward it. Our larger collective may be our cultural group, our family, people of the same race, people of the same gender, a professional group, or some other association. The majority in this reciprocal relationship may be vocal in their approval or disapproval of a group member's behavior. Consequently, an identity group can be a strong source of support and reassurance, but if you break the rules or go against expected norms, it can just as easily become a source of discomfort, stress, and loneliness. In addition, because identity groups typically form unofficial (but powerful) measurements of acceptable standards, they impose values or behaviors on their members, and these values and behaviors may be beneficial but they may also be skewed. For example, many black students are told by their peers that doing well in school is being too "white," so the contrary, doing poorly, becomes synonymous with being "black." Unfortunately for some black students, the consequence of this mind-set is a focus on activities other than academic endeavors.

Although a considerable part of what constitutes identity is revealed in our expression of belonging, an even greater part of our identity may be invisible to others. Each of us determines this aspect of identity as we consider to which group or groups we belong, what that belonging means to us, to whom we give our primary allegiance, and how our identity plays out in terms of our behaviors, beliefs, and values. Other people may think they have gathered a clear understanding of our identity from our visible expressions, but sometimes—because identity can be too personal to share or too controversial—we may choose to hide our true selves from their inquisitive eyes.

Further complicating the concept of identity is human variability. Some of us link our identity with our race, others with our class, gender, or geographical region. For many of us, our identity arises from a combination of things. But regardless of the associations with which it is intertwined, identity is a powerful force, one capable of influencing our behaviors, values, and attitudes—and one that often serves as a source of discomfort for African Americans in the corporate setting.

Identity issues are a fundamental force in the workplace, yet they tend to go unseen and unnamed by institutions and by people. Identity is a sticky area where organizations don't like to go; it is safer for them to promote color blindness, which inevitably favors the dominant culture. As a result, African Americans are frequently faced with having to choose only one or two aspects of their identity to acknowledge in the workplace. Black leaders faced with this forced choice tend to have one of these four responses: hiding their identity and assimilating or appearing to assimilate into the dominant workplace culture; struggling to balance the tensions between their workplace personas and individual identity; finding ways to express individual identity outside the workplace; and confronting black-on-black issues.

Assimilation and the Inability to Be Yourself

For many black leaders, questions of identity are tied up with complicated notions of acceptance in their work world. Some fear that any overt or unbridled expression of African American identity will jeopardize their position as a leader or their opportunity to rise to that level of responsibility. Others are not always certain how much of "themselves" they can or should express. "I cannot be totally me in the work environment," explains James Kelley, a sales specialist at a health-care products company. "Part of me is a black male and that would not be acceptable," he says, referring to aspects of his wit and sarcasm that stem from his black roots and may not be understood by others. "I have to put myself in a box that I think would be acceptable."

Although leaders such as Kelley stifle themselves to be "more acceptable" at work, others have attempted to transform themselves, to become, in essence, "intentionally assimilated." Says James Washington, a manager at a major chemical company, "I knew I had to incorporate myself into that culture. And I said, 'I can do it either one or two ways. I can try to incorporate myself into this culture and be successful, or I can let them know that, "hey, I ain't listening to no jokes about so and so and so."' . . . So I gave a lot of myself, I gave—sometimes I gave so much of myself that I had to go home and look in the mirror. Because sometimes I was deeply hurt, deeply pained. I felt like I was sacrificing the thing that meant the most to me—my blackness." In order to be a success at work, Washington tried to integrate himself into the work culture so strongly that he believed other blacks saw him as one who had lost his racial identity. "The other part that was hurtful was that while I was trying to incorporate myself into that culture, I was, in a lot of ways, known as an 'Uncle Tom' to my peers." Ironically, when asked what it means to be black, Washington replies, "It means everything to me."

Kelley's and Washington's experiences are by no means unique. Our study revealed that more than 50 percent of black professionals surveyed believe they have had to give up some of their identity as an African American in order to effectively perform their jobs. Although blacks may often feel these sacrifices are necessary, they also often find them difficult to make.

The Identity Struggle

Even when they have not given so much of themselves that like James Washington they find their behaviors and values at odds, many blacks are aware that being black in corporate America can set their desired expressions of identity and their professional behaviors against each other. They see themselves as caught in a continuing struggle to maintain their racial identity while advancing their careers.

Nelson Evans, a manager at a national pharmacy organization, describes the fight he believes is waged every day. "There is an identity struggle, trying to remember, keep abreast of who you are." Helen Thompson, a program manager at a major chemical company, describes what can happen when you are the only black or one of the few in a workplace. "It is very easy for a black person to lose themselves in the [work] environment. It's dominated by white people, and then you begin to question who you are." Monica Stewart, team leader at a medical research organization, also talks about maintaining her identity as if it were a constant battle. "I think that part of the struggle that we face with this is where can I go to have identity? Where can I go and say, 'Oh, my God, they look like me. It's OK. I'm not the only one.'"

Not surprisingly, the language many people use to describe this conflict is one of battle: the struggle, the fight, the war. Perhaps it is because what's at stake in this conflict—one's sense of self—has such serious consequences if lost.

Finding a Place to Be Who You Are

Other leaders, recognizing that it may be difficult or impossible to exhibit their identity as blacks in the work world, feel they must find some form of expression if they are going to survive in corporate America. The safest forms of expression for many are those that take place outside the workplace, in traditionally black spheres or neighborhoods.

Robert Stanley, a vice president in an international polling agency, speaks about living in a white community and taking extreme measures to keep in contact with his black roots. "I went twenty miles to find a black church. I had a long-distance relationship. In order to remain the person that I am, I would go through extraordinary means for a short period of time. It's extremely difficult to be an African American in America—to be able to escape whites. It's very easy for whites to escape blacks." Without periodic infusions of black culture, Stanley says he would go "crazy." The fact that other blacks have echoed Stanley's sentiments about finding full security and support only through a sense of connection to a black community is telling for these professionals who so often feel disconnected at work.

The desire to maintain their sense of identity is one of the reasons some African Americans find networking with other blacks crucial to their work experience. Along with such work-related benefits as sharing information and insights, such networking provides an opportunity to rehearse one's culture and spend time with other black people. As a colleague of ours once explained, he comes by our offices when he needs to "get his black fix." Because many blacks work in environments where they are the only black person or have just a few black colleagues, connecting with other African Americans helps stave off their cultural loneliness and fear of losing their identity in the workplace.

But How Black Are You?

In a dynamic unique to African Americans, part of the difficulty for black leaders in being fully who they are at work arises out of their relationships with other African Americans. Although one's racial group can be a source of extreme comfort, it can also impose its own expectations and standards of acceptance. For example, one man we interviewed continually referred to a black colleague as "the white black guy." In giving his colleague this label, this man assumed he had both the right to judge another's level of "blackness" and the authority to find that coworker lacking. In addition, by sharing this nickname with others, he was actively challenging his colleague's identity and encouraging criticism and ostracism of that colleague by other blacks in the office.

When asked about such counterproductive behaviors, Jamaal Laker, an HR consultant at a national insurance company, says he has seen them all in action before. "I don't have those types of hang-ups, nor am I what I call a 'soul patrol' person, who dictates, 'well, he's African American but he prefers to listen to rock rather than hip-hop, therefore he ain't really black, and he speaks perfect English and uses slang generally associated with whites as opposed to blacks.'" So, although not all people take it upon themselves to scrvc as judge and jury for their brothers' and sisters' measure of correct identity, this behavior (and the fear of it) looms in the corporate setting as yet another divisive aspect, adding to the prevailing miasma.

What many African American leaders have come to understand is that one's identity is not linked solely to race, nor should it be. This means that some black managers choose other equally significant values as a basis for their actions. For example, people's religious affiliations, professional responsibilities, skills, status, and even their personal ambition can motivate their behaviors, behaviors that may then be considered outside the acceptable norm as it is established by others. Colin Powell, who has been simultaneously extolled and vilified by the black community, is a case in point. Although no one but Powell himself can state categorically what his drivers are, it is clear that they have motivated him to become a political powerhouse in a Republican administration—an alliance generally deemed outside the African American mainstream. Ultimately, if you allow others (or yourself) to use race as the sole motivation for making decisions or for determining the patterns of your life, you reduce yourself to a one-dimensional being. You deny yourself the full expression and complexity of your humanity.

By defining what constitutes "acceptable black behavior," many African Americans limit the ways they perform and the ways they think about things. Although many blacks may rail at others for doing this, it is sadly ironic that they also do it to themselves. Consider Marcella Watkins, whose story began this chapter, and her dilemma: wearing a wig or sporting her naturally short hair. Her struggle was rooted in a societal beauty myth perpetuated by her mother, which she then internalized for herself. Her story keenly illustrates the key to identity issues in the workplace: it is a person's *perception* of a situation that carries the impact, not necessarily the truth of the situation. Although the ramifications of such perceptions may be only indirectly related to job performance, they can have considerable impact on personal lives and self-esteem.

Why Identity Is Important

Understanding the dynamic that an identity of difference creates in the workplace is the first step to understanding the nuances of the unique challenges of black leadership. Identity issues affect black leaders every day, influencing everything from their personal dress decisions to their professional strategies and activities. The more black leaders' identity differences can be acknowledged and respected the more the door is opened to leveraging their perspectives in ways that benefit them as leaders and the companies and communities in which they work.

Compounding Stress

Being unsure whether you can wear a certain outfit or a particular hairstyle to work may seem fairly unimportant. However, if you are black, it becomes yet another aspect of your work persona that must be carefully considered before being acted upon and presented to the world at large. Sometimes others may invest innocent behaviors with political meanings that can have career-altering ramifications. Blacks often feel that whites are sizing up their professional potential and suitability by how closely they fit or emulate white middle-class norms.

One black man we talked with said that he never discussed politics at work because as one of few blacks at a largely white, conservative organization he believed that his views, combined with his race, would limit his "promotability." Another woman discussed how she once wanted to change her hairstyle from relaxed to cornrows, just for something different, but after discussing it with her family and black work colleagues, she decided that the potential risk to her career was just too great.

In our conversations with black managers, we have heard many stories recounting similar dilemmas. Whether it springs from something as ingrained as identity or as seemingly shallow as fashion, each situation requires the same consideration: whether or not one can act or should act. These considerations add to the stress that African Americans already feel at work. Even if they decide to proceed with their perceived "Afro-centric" behavior and even if they are not penalized for it at work, the stress that stems from having to engage in these considerations—the feeling that you are always on the defensive—is wearing. Beverly Tatum, author of *Why Are All the Black Kids Sitting Together in the Cafeteria?* agrees: "Whether one succumbs to the devaluing pressures of the dominant culture or successfully resists them, the fact is that dealing with oppressive systems from the underside, regardless of the strategy, is physically and psychologically taxing."

Valuing Different Perspectives

As individuals and as corporate leaders, it is important for us all to recognize the value of African American perspectives. The opportunity to express one's identity at work leads to opportunities to educate and broaden the knowledge of others. Brad Harold, a senior vice president at a major financial institution, explains, "As the only black at the table, I know what I have to offer is valuable. I bring a different perspective and I bring a different tone."

People who bring a different perspective to the workplace and help others to see it do more than help to teach others, they can also use that perspective when making business decisions. For example, people with minority perspectives have unique insight into the growing markets of minority communities. They can also help the management that sees a problem from one perspective to find a new framework. In the Walter Kaitz Foundation documentary film *Reinventing America,* John Bryant, executive director of Operation Hope, explains, "You *can* do well and do good. You can do well *by* doing good. Bringing blacks and browns and women onto your board of directors is not something you do because it looks nice. It's the right thing to do because it's good business.

It is something that is not only morally right, but is also economically smart."

In addition, at a time when employee retention is a major concern, the willingness of an organization to respect an employee's identity can be a powerful retention tool.

Understanding How African Americans Are Perceived

Exploring how identity is viewed in the workplace may help blacks understand how others perceive them. Janet Matthews, a staff nurse at a Massachusetts hospital, says, "When I get up in the morning and look in the mirror, I don't get up and see a 'black woman.' I get up in the morning and say, 'you need to do something to your hair,' et cetera. And it is not until somebody else does something to make you realize that you're black, that you become conscious of being black."

Difference exists only when we have something to contrast it with. Tatum notes that "the parts of identity that do capture our attention are those that other people notice and reflect back to us." Individuals can use this reflection, which tells them what is considered different from the norm, to better see and understand aspects of African American culture that their organizations find "problematic." These reflections can help them decide whether corporate attitudes or responses to black employees are reasonable and have true implications for the business or whether they are knee-jerk reactions that come from being uncomfortable with someone who is different. Knowing the difference informs the decisions individuals make about their personal demeanor in the workplace.

Developing Inner Strength

People who are comfortable with their identity are seemingly able to pull strength from that comfort. In our own work, we have found this concept particularly important for African Americans because their belief in self, despite the many struggles that surround being black, gives them the courage and strength to face the corporate world.

"I just cherish and love my blackness," says Keith Shields, a senior vice president at a financial institution. "It's given me power to be noticed. It's given me opportunity." Brad Harold echoes this sentiment of turning difference into advantage. "I believe my blackness gives me a twenty-second advantage in every situation I walk into. People pay attention to me, if only because I'm different." Dorothy Summit, an account manager at a major chemical company, says she is proud of being black and that her heritage gives her goals and a *center*—a fulcrum from which she can leverage herself. "When I think of [being black], it's kind of knowing who I am, having a center, and making this the best I can be. That's just what I think of when I think of belonging to the group."

Too often whites and others believe that African Americans find being black only a trial or a burden. Although challenges certainly exist, they are by no means the entire story. Being black, being different, also brings its unique share of joys, pleasures, and strengths. Difference can help African Americans in the workplace, serving as a reservoir from which to draw perseverance and inner strength.

What Is Unique to the Black Experience

The most notable facet of the issue of racial identity in the workplace is that for whites, it is not an issue. Certainly, ethnic identity, religious identity, and other forms of cultural identity are important to large numbers of people, but identity based on race is not normally a conscious consideration for those who look like the majority. This is largely because expressions of the majority group's identity and norms are already incorporated into the workplace culture. The hairstyles, clothing, manner of joking and expressing oneself—in short, most of the values and behaviors whites are used to—are already incorporated into, and thus deemed appropriate by, the corporate world. In general, white professionals do not have to think (or fret) about expressing their white identity because it is taken for granted. They do not have to worry about losing their whiteness or leaving it at the door when they come to work. Because they are white, they fit in—identity and all—in a way that African Americans and other ethnic and racial minorities cannot.

Figure 2.1 summarizes one of the difficulties with identity that blacks experience in the office environment. In our survey, only 46 percent responded that their identity as blacks is respected or valued in the workplace. Perhaps part of the reason for this is that because whites do not have to consider identity in the same way that other groups do, they may not see the significant challenges for others who attempt to express their identity in the workplace and thus do not recognize the value and importance of those expressions.

FIGURE 2.1. Identity and African Americans.

Less than half of African American leaders believe their identity is respected and valued in their jobs.

Biculturalism

Most traditionally disempowered groups deal with being *bicultural,* meaning that they must move back and forth between two distinct cultural worlds, their own and that of the dominant group. Learning to comfortably traverse two cultures without giving up one's identity entirely is a necessary skill if a black leader is to succeed in corporate America without losing his or her sense of self. "We have to know how to live in two cultures," says Jamaal Laker. "We have to be able to hang in the 'hood with the folks, and we also have to be able to go to work in a setting where 98 percent of the people will be white and from a different culture."

Biculturalism takes its toll on black professionals, regardless of the sphere they are moving in at the moment. In *Our Separate Ways: Black and White Women and the Struggle for Professional Identity*, Ella Edmondson Bell and Stella Nkomo examined the bicultural experiences of seventy-one African American, career-oriented women. They found that "for African American women, biculturality, or moving from one cultural context to another, requires that they shape their careers in the white world, while shaping other dimensions of their life in the black community. Bicultural stress is a concomitant psychological barrier black professional women feel when they are compelled to suppress or diminish one part of their identity in order to exist in either of the cultural contexts where they work or live."

An especially critical aspect of biculturalism seems to be the attitude people take toward the culture that is not their own. For some, particularly those who have a very defined view of what it is to be an African American, adopting some aspects of another culture or learning how to navigate in that culture is a "giving up" of who they are. For others, such behaviors become a way to grow. We have been struck by the number of black managers in CCL's African-American Leadership Program who ask, in effect, Why must we always be the ones to change or adapt? Why don't whites have to make some allowances sometime?

Children: The Next Generation

Yet another facet of the identity question for many African American leaders concerns not themselves but their children. Many black corporate leaders live in white neighborhoods, largely because of their financial and social success, and so have concerns about what this decision and lifestyle may mean for their families over the long run. They struggle with the ways their families will be influenced, affected, deprived, or overwhelmed by spending the major-ity of their time and energies in a culture that reflects little (if any) of their own identity.

Mark Hammer, a senior manager who lives in a largely white suburb ("I would prefer to live in the city, but I live in the suburbs"), expresses concerns about the limited influences on his children and says that he is "very sensitive . . . to the fact that my kids are in a predominantly white school." Dorothy Summit and her husband go out of their way to keep their child connected to the black com-munity. "Having a daughter to raise," she says, "my husband and I have to make sure that she has a sense of who she is."

This concern about their children's identity adds a special stress for parents who view the material benefits they have given their children as blessings, but wonder what consequential effects on their children's identity these lifestyles may invoke. Furthermore, many believe they must work extra hard to prepare their children for the struggle they will encounter once they move beyond the protective environments their parents have created for them—for they, one day soon, will enter into a corporate environment that may not yet be fully open to those who look different.

What You as African Americans Can Do

Ultimately, identity is a deeply personal, complex equation. For those of you who are black leaders, it is critical that you understand the power of your identity and the nuances it holds for you, both in and out of the workplace. Here are suggestions for deepening your understanding of the impact that identity issues have in your life. Understanding this impact allows you to make the best, most informed choices for your individual circumstances—for your val-ues, your goals, your current workplace, and your career.

Expand your ideas about identity. African Americans must be will-ing to expand their notions of what is acceptable. They should recognize that being black is not what they *do*, but who they *are*. There is irony in that as blacks fight for more opportunities, many other blacks then castigate those who take these opportunities. African Americans today have a wide spectrum of backgrounds. Many have been raised in middle- or upper-class circumstances. Some have been raised in other countries. Some come from two-parent homes, some from single-parent homes. They bring a variety of experiences to the table, and no single one of them is the definitive treatise for all blacks or the primary source of blacks' individual or collective identity.

African Americans raised in the inner city or the rural South are not just "black." They may be rich blacks, poor blacks, light-skinned blacks, or dark-skinned blacks; they may like R&B, they may prefer jazz, or they may even like country and western. Although this may sound like the kind of categorizing found in a Dr. Seuss book, the fact remains that one can't label or limit blacks—or any other group for that matter—because the world is full of *individuals*. No matter how each African American chooses to define his or her blackness, blacks will find themselves the richer if they acknowledge all these many kinds of blackness, rather than alienating those they have difficulty relating to and shutting them out of the group.

Determine what identity means for you. It's important to determine what identity means for you personally. Keep in mind that just because you as an African American hold a particular point of view, that doesn't make your view a black issue. The content of an issue is what makes it a black issue. Also recognize that identity is expressed in different ways by different people. What some people feel is integral to their identity, others see as unimportant behaviors or needless distractions. The difference between identity and style, for example, is in the eye of the beholder *and* the wearer. Two people can have the same behaviors but those behaviors can mean very different things.

One woman we know explained that when she got her ears pierced for a second time, the multiple-pierced-ear look was seen mostly on black women. Consequently, when she went for a job

---

What African Americans Can Do About Identity

Expand your ideas about identity.

Determine what identity means for you.

Inventory your expressions of identity.

Consider your behaviors before acting.

---

interview, she took the second earring out, considering it simply a fashion statement. Another young woman pierced her ears twice and complemented the look with a nose ring. She swore, however, that she would not take her rings out for job interviews because they were a part of her identity—a part of who she was. "If the job can't handle them, [the organization] can't handle me," she said. These two women are friends, and yet their expressions of identity, in this instance at least, are very different. Either could accuse the other of inappropriately expressing herself—one for "selling out" and the other for overtly overexpressing her freedom.

Conversely, Wilson Davis, a lead systems technical specialist at a tobacco company, recalled the time when a white coworker and friend told him that he was smarter than a lot of his black colleagues and that he didn't have to do "stupid" things like wearing dashikis and a twelve-inch afro. Davis's friend pulled him aside and said, "If you want the job, you have to do the job. If you want to survive where whites are in the majority, you have to look like they look to get along." Davis chose to accept this advice. For him the issue was not one of identity but survival. "I decided to stop competing and to be more wily. Instead of having foes, I now had coworkers. A lot of blacks in the company took a long time to figure this out. They were held back or left the company." Davis did not feel as if he were sacrificing his identity by following his friend's suggestions. Instead, he saw himself as taking strategic means to secure his job and even made friends with those who (he perceived) had not originally intended to befriend a black man.

Inventory your expressions of identity. As you determine what identity means for you, take an inventory of the ways you express your identity and consider your motivations for each expression. Consider how you express identity at home and in your personal and professional communities. These expressions might take the form of dress and physical appearance, the language you use in conversations, your time investment, and so forth. What expressions do you feel are appropriate in each place, and why? What does each workplace expression cost you and what do you gain by it? Are you making any sacrifices as a result of expressing your identity or stifling it? Ask yourself, Why am I doing the things I'm doing? Are you going along with the crowd or reacting without thinking? Make sure you choose your identity issues consciously, by making decisions after considering all the ramifications of your actions. At least go in knowing the price of your decisions.

If you cannot fully be yourself at work, consider the venues where you can celebrate and express your identity: for example, your neighborhood, church, volunteer work, professional affiliation group, and service group. Where do you go to be fully yourself? Where do you get "your black fix"?

Consider your behaviors before acting. Whatever the expression of identity and the circumstance, it is important that you know what the issue is, what the expression means for you, and what the potential consequences of that expression might be. For example, one man we interviewed told us how he walked out of high school in the ninth grade in protest because the administration wouldn't permit a Muslim speaker for the Black Heritage Club. However, at that time, he didn't know what a Muslim was, he just wanted to be accepted by his larger group and saw this as a way of gaining acceptance. Instead, he ended up getting suspended and having to deal with an irate mother. Later he learned that her ire came less from his suspension than from his taking a stance to support a value that he neither understood nor believed. Many blacks may find themselves facing similar choices in the workplace. If you are going to take an action or make a stand, make sure the issue is meaningful to you personally, not just to those around you. Ask yourself, Do I need to express myself this way? and, Are there other ways of making this point effectively? Make sure you understand what you are trying to accomplish with your behavior; you may need to question your motivation behind the proposed action. In addition, be clear about the possible consequences of your actions and be ready to accept them if they come.

What You as Colleagues Can Do

As the workmate of African Americans, perhaps the most challenging but most important thing you can do is to *see* their struggle with the miasma of difference. Heightening your awareness of identity issues means recognizing what they mean to others and to yourself. It means looking at "the norm" with open eyes and without assumptions.

Be alert to identity issues. As a manager, a colleague, and a leader, it is important that you try to fully consider the identity issues faced by African Americans. The time when these issues seem contrary or confusing to you is perhaps the most important time to listen without judgment. If you are white, recognize that most non-whites receive subtle messages from both the work and national cultures that their identity is not as valuable as yours. Thus they may be more cognizant of identity questions than you are because they are apt to have to deal with more questions about their identity. If you are another person of color, recognize that your group may have identity concerns similar to those of your black colleagues. Although these issues may not be identical, they usually involve feeling less than whole in the workplace. We suggest that you respect African American identity issues, just as we urge blacks to respect yours. Together you can create support groups so that more of your issues concerning identity are addressed and respected.

Examine your assumptions about identity. Assumptions about identity frame individuals' communications and interactions both when they are with people different from them and when they are with their own group. Consider the most important components or formative elements of your identity: Do they spring from aspects of life you have inherited or ones you have chosen? How do they play out or find expression in your home life, your community, and your professional spheres? Have you ever considered race to be a part of your identity, and why or why not? Lastly, consider the experiences you have had with African Americans and people of color in your community, your neighborhood, and your workplace. What similarities do you share with these individuals, and what are the differences you notice?

Realize that black-raised doesn't always mean black-related. The difficulty of distinguishing between racial and non-racial issues can cause major misunderstandings in the workplace and people can become unnecessarily polarized. Just as white people may champion causes that are not race related, black people may raise issues that have no underlying racial meaning. Sometimes, however, because people are sensitive about racial issues, someone who is not black may feel obligated or pressured to see any issue as a black issue because its advocate is a black person. As a general guideline, consider an issue a black issue only if it deals with the needs of African American people.

Take an inventory of the unspoken norms in your department and workplace. The *unspoken norms* are the behavior patterns that implicitly or explicitly reflect corporate identity. For example, does your company or department have an implicit or explicit dress code? What are the norms for interpersonal communications? Are there informal groupings in the office, in the lunchroom, around the watercooler, for drinks after work, and so forth? If so, whom do these groups include, and how might these groups be exclusive?

What Colleagues Can Do About Identity

Be alert to identity issues.

Examine your assumptions about identity.

Realize that black-raised doesn't always mean black-related.

Take an inventory of the unspoken norms in your department and workplace.

Your goal is to raise your awareness of the effects of miasma on African American colleagues, to become aware of your work group's unspoken norms and also your own, and to learn how these norms play out in the workplace. Communicate this information. Consider sharing it with others in your organization, with the human resource department or with your team. Consider whether you want to be an advocate.

Having a sense of responsibility toward the African American community is an aspect of identity that shapes many black leaders' careers, influencing everything from long-range goals to daily activities. The successes many blacks achieve today have been made possible by the risks taken and the challenges met by those who have gone before them. Consequently, many blacks feel they are inextricably linked with and responsible to their forebears. We explore how this plays out in the workplace in the next chapter, "Looking Out for Each Other."

3

Looking Out for Each Other

I do feel I have a responsibility in my organization to help [African Americans] get an understanding of the cultural landscape and unspoken things that could derail them.

—Marcella Watkins, director in a major consulting firm

You don't forget where you come from. You help bring somebody else along. You have a moral obligation to bring somebody else. . . . In my pursuit of excellence, it's not all about me. If I don't do anything to ensure that opportunities exist for others, what have I done?

—Tyrone Billington, general manager of a public utility

I think it's an obligation you feel. It's an obligation that's probably the result of experiences you've had during your career and your desire to make it better. A desire to try to help. . . . It's very, very difficult to walk away from it. We have a few that can. I'm not sure how they manage to do it, but we have a few that can do it.

—Rita Farax, human resource director for a major chemical firm

The voices of these black managers echo the sentiments of the many African American professionals who feel that their professional responsibility is a mixture of work, personal duty, and racial obligation. The latter is a compelling result of their respect for and accountability to those who came before them and struggled to get them and other blacks into, among other things, corporate America. It includes a tacit agreement that they will, in turn, help those blacks who strive alongside them and those who will follow them. It is a responsibility that is felt keenly. In fact more than 90 percent of the African Americans we surveyed said they felt responsible for helping other African Americans in their organizations.

Furthermore, the idea of racial obligation goes beyond what is due to the legacy of one's predecessors. Most leaders we surveyed believe there is a link in the minds of their white colleagues between their job performance and that of other African Americans. Nearly 90 percent say that if they are successful in their jobs, other African Americans will be seen in a better light. Around 50 percent also believe their non-black colleagues generalize the mistakes of one African American to all African Americans. Consequently, many blacks carry the burden of believing that if they fail or if their efforts are intensely scrutinized by whites and are judged to be lacking, others will suffer. Conversely, they also believe that their success will help determine whether other blacks are given opportunities or are intensely scrutinized by whites. Robert Stanley, vice president of a major polling firm, summed it up this way: "If I fall and stumble, as I often do, other African Americans are adversely affected. Senior managers and mid-managers are risk averse. Africans Americans are still seen as being a risk."

For black managers, responsibilities are not solely about race. But being black may color the manner in which their responsibilities play out, organizationally and personally. For African Americans, carrying out these responsibilities links what they believe they owe each other with what they think is due the organization. Consequently, the concept of responsibility can easily turn into a burden for those who feel they must play the part of "the racial representative" of the organization. Whether African Americans accept this racial responsibility or not, the fact that it exists is stressful—further complicating the miasma in which black managers must act. For everyone who seeks relief from the effect of miasma in the workplace, it is important to examine organizational and personal responsibilities and to illuminate how the responsibilities for blacks are similar to and different from the responsibilities that all managers share.

What Being Responsible for Others Looks Like

Leaders' workplace responsibilities revolve around the duties or obligations that are due themselves, others, and the organization. An individual's sense of responsibility is influenced by internal and external factors. Those factors help to ensure that work gets done and they bind various work groups in the company together. However, leaders' having a sense of responsibility does not always mean a positive outcome for the organization. Employees who feel they are responsible to a cause that is opposed to the organization's interests can certainly cause problems, as can individuals who feel responsible only to themselves. For African American leaders, traditional job responsibilities may come wrapped in a blanket of miasma, which convolutes conditions or acceptance for blacks' behavior, performance, and ability to feel and be considered successful. The notion of success may appear different for blacks and non-blacks.

Organizational Responsibilities

In general, organizational responsibilities are the behaviors and activities that most organizations believe are inherent in their "contract" with their employees. These duties serve as general measuring sticks for individuals' competency as workers and managers. Because African American leaders often feel they should shoulder additional, race-related responsibilities or are asked to do so, the burden of their organizational duties can be more demanding than that of traditional leaders. Organizational responsibilities can be broken down into task, team, and leadership responsibilities.

Task Responsibilities. Task responsibilities entail performing well in both primary and additional job duties, such as completing projects with timeliness, accuracy, and quality. Excelling at task-oriented responsibilities is the cornerstone for building credibility and a reputation for sterling work. Although most people think of these efforts as simply accomplishing the tasks at hand, the responsibilities that surround "getting the job done" ultimately contribute to organizational effectiveness. Task responsibilities for African Americans are marked by the pressures of having to work twice as hard, represent other blacks, maintain rigid emotional control, and compensate for additional race-related tasks.

For people of color, task responsibilities are where the issue of working twice as hard to receive the same credit first arises. People of color often say they have to work harder than whites if they want to get ahead. If they do not work extra hard or have extra qualifications, they believe their competency and credibility will suffer. Tyrone Billington explains his frustration at having to have a graduate degree for his job when his white peers do not. "For an African American male, you have to have that education. The first thing they [ask] when they look at you is, 'Is he competent?' Our white counterparts aren't pressured to be competent. They don't have to prove themselves." Billington's comments echo sentiments of many other blacks who feel pressured to become overqualified in an effort to compete "equally" with whites.

Not everyone supports the belief that blacks have to work twice as hard to get ahead. Richard F. America and Bernard E. Anderson say, in *Soul in Management,* that this notion is "a myth that persists unexamined and unchallenged." Yet David Thomas and John Gabarro, in their book *Breaking Through,* document how minorities who eventually became executives had to prove themselves over longer periods of time than their white counterparts before they received the opportunity to move ahead. Interestingly, Thomas and Gabarro also show that after putting in significantly more time in the trenches, minority leaders eventually mirrored their white counterparts' progression once they approached the executive ranks.

One implication is that because the establishment bias favors traditional managers, mediocre white managers may get into the executive circle more easily than their minority colleagues. The stringent criteria applied to minority managers makes it less likely that any but the most able, ambitious, and persistent minority managers reach the executive level. Says Nan Blunt, a manager for an executive development firm, "We have all the African Americans in leadership roles. We have all these black superstars—we don't hire just plain ol' average black folks. . . . I often experience the support of African Americans who are the select few. There are other people who need support too. I wonder about what support there is for people in certain parts of the organization. I wonder about people in entry-level positions."

Whether blacks actually have to work harder than their white colleagues to get ahead may be difficult to prove or disprove. What is clear is that a large number of blacks perceive this to be the reality, and consequently they feel under constant pressure to establish and maintain their credibility. Helen Thompson, a manager at a chemical company, feels she has to be as close to perfect as possible because others are waiting for her to falter. "It's a tremendous burden," she says, "that you feel you always have to excel and others don't have that [pressure]." Companies may lose nontraditional workers with potential because they simply get tired of "swimming in the same pool."

For many leaders this pressure is increased by their belief that to fail undermines not only themselves but also other African Americans, whom they are seen as representing. Thus the notion of success—and of working twice as hard to achieve it—becomes loaded with the responsibility for others' future. "I can't accept failure for myself," says Jan Henry, another manager at a chemical company, "because when I fail at something, I feel like it is more than me somehow that has failed, or at least that's how the world is going to view it."

Yet despite the additional stress of feeling daily scrutiny and pressure to succeed, many black leaders also believe they must retain a high level of "coolness" on the job. They are required to control their emotions and to express them in ways that do not seem out of control to their white counterparts. Studies by CCL suggest that the range of behaviors considered acceptable for African Americans is narrower than the range allowed to their white colleagues. Consequently, if blacks lose their temper or show what seems to be excessive passion about an idea, their emotion is considered out of control, even if it mirrors the accepted behaviors of a white employee. James Washington, a chemical company manager, says that he has to be extra sensitive and aware of the feelings of others in his office. "I can't get pissed off. I can't jump up and say . . . 'What the hell is wrong, you know we can't have that,' and so forth. I see my white counterparts with the same kind of project have the same kind of anger, get pissed off, throw the chair, slam the phone, tell folks that if they don't get their asses right there, they'll fire their asses, and so forth. I can't do that. . . . I have to always be in control of my emotions." Although we do not condone these particular behaviors as appropriate for any manager and neither does Washington, others and CCL research also suggest that the repercussions for whites who behave outside the norm are not as stringent as those for blacks.

One African American manager in a consulting firm dealt with peers who were constantly challenging him for what they considered inaccuracies in his team's work. When they would call him and rant and rave about the shoddy work of his department, he calmly tried to explain the events leading to his decisions. He was told he was being defensive and that he should cool down and express himself differently. When subsequent events showed that his department's work was not shoddy and that in fact he had been correct, his colleagues apologized only rarely. In these interactions it was the black manager who was deemed to have the responsibility of keeping emotions in check, not his white counterparts.

For African American leaders, then, task responsibilities go well beyond those due the organization; they include managing the perceptions that their white coworkers hold about them as individuals and as members of a race. The common outcome of this responsibility is stress, yet because it is generally unseen by whites, this kind of stress generally goes undiscussed in open forums, leaving many African Americans to talk about it among themselves and to manage it as well as they can.

On top of these expectations they have of themselves, black managers are often given special tasks by their organizations, such as taking care of blacks and black issues, as a matter of course. These tasks may include mentoring other blacks and networking with or speaking up for newer or less well-known blacks in the company. Although organizations reap benefits when African American leaders assume these responsibilities, these assignments are usually given over and above their normal job requirements and therefore do not count toward promotions or result in "brownie points" of any kind.

One former college professor recalls opening her mailbox on her first day on the job to find that although no one had inquired about her interests, she had been assigned to recruit black students. Less than a week later, two black students came by her office to introduce themselves. They were not her students, nor were they likely to be, but their white male professor had sent them upstairs to meet her. He meant no ill intent, but he had mistakenly assumed that although these were his students, she would become their main liaison for information and support and be available to them for any number of other issues.

Although many African Americans take on these responsibilities because of their own sense of what they should do, to *expect* them to do so is problematic. Such expectations, especially when they come from the corporation, deny individuals a choice about the kinds of responsibilities that are seen as discretionary for others, foisting upon them duties they may not want for a variety of reasons and may not be prepared to handle. On a deeper level these expectations suggest that the individual is being viewed, probably uncon-sciously, largely as a *black* employee rather than as an employee who, because she is black, may have some knowledge in these areas. The distinction lies in making assumptions about a black employee versus seeking her input about her skills, availability, and interest.

Team Responsibilities. Beyond their responsibilities connected with the specific tasks of a job, all leaders are also accountable to the team with whom they work. This means they must give their boss, peers, direct reports, and clients (both internal and external) timely and accurate information. It also means they must lend support to teammates when needed. Further, the idea of team responsibilities may be expanded to include providing exemplary customer service to internal and external clients, in an effort to ensure that people are satisfied and that the larger organization runs more smoothly.

African American leaders sometimes find team responsibilities challenging, not because they don't understand team dynamics but because they're not always sure of their standing within the team. In many circumstances blacks question whether they are viewed as full and equal partners on the team. Jan Henry says that when she works with people, they have to decide if she is worthy of the posi-tion. "So I start behind any white manager in any position. . . . While I am trying to gain confidence, my white counterpart is six months down the road. Maybe not that far, but the point is that we have to . . . do a lot of scrambling in order to stay even because of this early confidence piece." Eileen Bender, a sales manager at a large telecommunications company, remembered when she had a technical assignment and a teammate who, she perceived, did not think that she belonged on the project. This teammate, a white man, had an office where he could keep an eye on Bender—which he did. He did not, however, speak to or acknowledge her. "At the conclusion of my project, which won me accolades," Bender said, "he finally smiled at me and talked to me. Apparently, I had to earn the respect that would have been and was given automatically to others, [to] whites."

Often it is the uncertainty of acceptance when entering a team situation that proves difficult to bear. On one hand, assuming that the group will treat you as a leader or an equal partner (whichever the case may be) can set you up for failure. On the other hand, assuming that the group will not treat you equally can do the same thing, because people might see you as having a chip on your shoulder. Finding the balance between defensiveness and openness, being overachieving and being unacceptably perfectionist is difficult. Also, the point of balance changes with each new team you join. Thus lessons from a previous team may not transfer to a new team. On top of all this, increasingly people are being asked to work in teams, and these teams more often include people from various parts of the company. Although this shift may benefit the organizations, it means that African Americans face additional challenges as they work to gain equal status on increasing numbers and types of teams.

Beyond the issue of simple equity in status, black leaders sometimes question whether they are on a team because of their skill sets or because the team needed a minority presence. Even when black leaders are invited onto a team for their skills, others may reduce that invitation to the issue of race. "Well," one man said when a black female team leader was chosen for his group, "they must have needed a black woman." With one sentence this team member stripped the team leader of her skills and experience, minimizing her to her racial and gender status.

In other instances African Americans may find themselves being overly scrutinized. One black director in a service organization reported how the human resource department investigated him after he fired an employee. He recounted that the person who was fired had been on probation, was not coming to work on time, and was not doing a good job while there. Ultimately the investigation proved the firing was appropriate. However, before that investigation was complete, HR expanded it to examine other aspects of this director's managerial practices. Eventually, HR found the director's practices to be stellar.

For African American leaders the team environment is fraught with minefields. It can be hard to determine one's official responsibilities, and whether these responsibilities apply only to the black team member or are binding on all members of the team. For instance, do you owe loyalty to someone on the team who does not acknowledge your contributions? At what point do you stop trying to prove that you are worthy of team membership? How do you learn to trust and to let down the barriers that have long protected you? Clearly there are no pat answers. Each leader must determine the most effective course of action for each situation. The best answers come with organizational knowledge and self-understanding. Because each situation is different, the appropriate solution comes from being able to analyze each situation on its own merits.

Leadership Responsibilities. Leaders in an organization are expected to have a vision and then plan, organize, control, and direct people around that vision. In so doing they set a climate that allows them to develop and empower those working for them. For many African Americans, leadership responsibilities extend to issues of black representation, or the lack thereof, in the corporate worldview.

Many African Americans must contend with the unwillingness of coworkers to see them as leaders. They must cope with direct reports or peers who tend to work around them rather than with them. Some feel that because they are in leadership positions, they must speak for all blacks or all people of color. "Because I'm a director, I have a voice," says Marcella Watkins, "a voice I lend to Africans Americans, women, and other underrepresented groups." Still others believe they should play the role of change agent. Numerous leaders have told us stories of how they created networking groups or other race-based organizations in their companies as a way of supporting each other, defining their issues, and taking those issues to the company's top management. Robert Simpson, an account executive at a utility company, notes that people often seek him out to lead efforts to fix things in the company. "I see myself as a change agent in the company," he says. "I accept that responsibility. Sometimes I can enjoy it because I can see some progress. Other times it makes me angry and bitter and I have to work hard to, spiritually, not let those things . . . destroy me."

Some African American leaders believe they must be ready to help the organization and themselves when their company is ready to move toward more diversity. Bob Spring, a manager at a national retail company, tries to always be prepared, so that if the company is ready to move a minority employee into a new position, he not only can step in, but can do so and be effective in the role. "I don't just want to step in there and be that black guy they brought in there because he was black, and he didn't have a clue to what he was doing and blew it and ruined the opportunity for the next black person who comes along," he says. Whereas Spring is ready to use himself to create organizational change, Robert Stanley helps effect change by working hard to bring minority vendors into his organization. "If I don't, nobody else will," he says, adding, "In a weird way it's my responsibility to the company. It doesn't occur to them that the best [person] may be a person of color. . . . It's absolutely a good business decision. In our company, even though we don't realize it, it gives us a competitive advantage. There are experiences that we've had that we [can bring to clients] as consultants that others can't provide." Stanley's comment underscores how leaders in many organizations find it difficult to picture people of color as being among the best. Consequently, when people of color are brought into an organization, many managers question their competence. Although many white managers may not assume a person of color comes from the bottom of the barrel, they are also not apt to believe that person comes from the top. That shortsighted assumption keeps many companies from finding and reaping the benefits of working with the best. It also causes these companies to overlook good people in house.

For African Americans the responsibilities around task, team, and leadership can be a source of support or of stress—an organizational benefit or detriment. For many blacks the ideas of not letting the race down and of helping the organization recognize and appreciate people and opportunities that are normally not seen by the organizational lens are key. What is not always evident, however, is that these two ideas are not mutually exclusive and in fact often support each other.

Personal Responsibilities

Alongside organizational responsibilities, all leaders have personal responsibilities that affect how they interact with and lead others. These responsibilities address the three arenas of individuals' personal lives: self, family, and community. Responsibilities in each arena can have a significant impact on how people conduct themselves at work.

Self-Responsibilities. Most leaders approach work with a strong sense of self-responsibility. For some it springs from an intrinsic motivation: their sense of self demands they do their best work whether or not others are watching. For others it is driven by their desire for external validation: for example, "I'm doing this because it is my job. I will be evaluated on this work. I will get promoted or be exposed to other opportunities if I do the work well."

Although blacks and non-blacks may use a similar process to internalize and externalize ideas of self-responsibility, they usually have different catalysts for their actions. Although these catalysts are not polar opposites, they can differ enough to render them opaque or obscure to the other group. And when the catalyst behind responsible behaviors is different from one's own norm, it can make the behaviors themselves appear more unfamiliar than they really are. This may mean that in certain instances some whites may not be able to identify what blacks consider to be responsible behavior.

When asked how they viewed responsibility, some participants in our study explained that they feel strongly that they should reach out to newer or less experienced blacks in the organization. This determination seems to come from a belief that this is simply something they should do. Often this desire to touch base takes the form of acclimating new black hires to make sure they know the lay of the land. Tom April, an HR specialist for a national brewery, said he and a colleague make sure to meet anyone of color who comes into the organization. Usually April has lunch with them and takes that opportunity to "coach them on things to look for and not to look for." Marcella Watkins likes to help new people get "the understanding of the cultural landscape and unspoken things that could derail them."

Joanna Gayle, a vice president at a major national bank, also takes young professionals under her wing. For example, when an African American man who was participating in an internlike program called her on a Friday, she returned his call at eight o'clock that evening and talked to him about what he would be doing and the company's expectations of him. When he came to work the next Tuesday, she spoke with him again in more detail. Gayle admits that she might not have extended herself quite as far had the new employee not been an African American. "When I heard his voice and saw him, my mentoring mode kicked in. I wanted to do everything I could to ensure his success. I wanted to make sure he went to all the right meetings and made all of the right connections."

In some African American circles, there is potential for misinterpretation of such self-responsible actions. Some black coworkers may invest a leader's sense of self-responsibility with negative meaning. Blacks who strive to do well for the sake of doing well, for example, may be seen by other blacks as trying to be white. Although not a common castigation, such comments hurt, and they can create self-doubt. The pain in being called "white" springs from the implication that one has lost or denied one's identity. Of course the idea that only whites can or should hold themselves to a high level of excellence is not only erroneous but detrimental to all African Americans.

Family Responsibilities. More than at any time in the past, family obligations are having an effect on the work lives of men as well as women. Increasingly, men are finding that they too are responsible for taking the children to the doctor's or dentist's office and for attending school functions. These obligations are affecting their work routine, as they, like their female counterparts, have to juggle often competing obligations. When talking about issues he wished his organization paid closer attention to, Brad Harold, a senior vice president for a major financial institution, said, "Work-life balance is very high on my scale. My track record is pretty solid, but I push the limit in terms of my flexibility during the day. I want time with my family, so I bend to allow for this. So when the kids need extra time, I want the flexibility to take care of this. I want [the company] to be more mindful of this. I try to do the same thing for my employees so they don't have to make the decision between work and their families."

Although blacks are dealing with these issues, some are also dealing with an especially large set of familial obligations. Rather than having responsibility for just those in their natal and nuclear families, African Americans may be expected to show primary loyalties to others who play familial roles in their lives, such as aunts, uncles, cousins, or the woman down the street who helped raise them. These expectations stem from black cultural norms that extend the concept of family beyond the natal family. Consequently, a person may find himself at odds with the company when he needs to meet obligations to family members that company policy does not recognize.

Community Responsibilities. For years corporations have been involved in community service as a way of both giving back and creating a favorable public image. In the name of the company, employees are urged to give time, money, or skills to organizations such as the United Way or the American Red Cross. Or they're encouraged to participate in group activity programs with agencies such as Habitat for Humanity or Meals on Wheels. Although working with or giving to these organizations is rarely mandated, whether or not one participates in sanctioned service activities is visible to others. In their book *The Leadership Odyssey*, Carole Napolitano and Lida Henderson characterize this challenge for today's leaders as particularly "unnerving," because it pressures leaders to take on yet one more task along with their job, family, and personal responsibilities. Nevertheless, the price for neglecting any of these important facets of life, including community service, the authors conclude, can be devastating because there is more to life than just work. In spite of this cost, leaders often ignore the call to community service, just as they pay insufficient attention to personal health, because it is easy to be driven by work, where the "accountability is so high and rewards and punishments so immediate." Although Napolitano and Henderson argue that today's leaders ignore the responsibility of community service, many of today's black leaders do take on this additional duty.

Indeed, for many African Americans, giving back to the community is a critical responsibility. Audrey Edwards and Craig K. Polite describe that feeling in their book *Children of the Dream:* "African Americans are the ones most likely to feel that their success represents not so much a gain ill gotten as it does an IOU still outstanding." Success for many blacks carries with it an enormous obligation to remember from where they came. If they don't remember, others in the community are happy to remind them.

Deborah Carter, a manager at an international petroleum company, spoke of having her responsibility recalled to her by a friend with whom she had not talked in years: "He congratulated me on my promotion. Then . . . he got real serious and said, 'What are you doing to give back to the community?'" He reminded Carter of her background—of the father who had died when she was six, of the mother who had a third-grade education, and of the teacher who had taken the two of them to museums and given them exposure to many different ideas—and said, "you really owe it to the community to do something and give back and celebrate your success by helping somebody else."

Giving back to the community is a powerful notion in black culture. Therefore many African Americans feel it is their right to comment on another black's commitment to community. Although not every black professional may give back or feel the need to do so, most have been asked, scolded, or quietly maligned if they were not doing so, and most have at least considered whether they are under any obligation to give back. Although this kind of questioning is healthy for any community, it does add another level of tension and stress for African American leaders.

Blacks often give back to the community as much to assist their company as to assist their community. In our interviews, many people talked about joining boards or talking to the black community on their corporation's behalf. Community organizations such as Girl Scouts and Boy Scouts, churches, and various and sundry clubs have all become avenues for black professionals to work with others and to do it in the name of their company. However, says Carl Swanson, a manager at a major chemical company, no one at his company knows that he is doing this work and that he is thus supporting the company's community service vision. Because this work is done outside the office and at the impetus of the individual leader, it may not be recognized by the organization. Swanson explains, "Nobody recognizes that because they don't see you here late at night . . . you're off to some meeting . . . playing a role that is necessary really for the company's vision." He also sees a solution: "We need to get some corporate understanding, first of all, on what the networking community activities bring to [the company]. Nobody's really willing to pay for something [when] they don't understand what it is they're paying for or getting out of it. And so, we probably need to be a little bit more direct with trying to understand exactly what we are getting out of it and what we expect from people in these [service] roles."

What Is Unique to the Black Experience

Some of the responsibilities that blacks undertake in the organization are expansions of those taken on by other leaders. Other behaviors, however, seem to be unique to the general black experience, or at least to the non-white experience. As we've stated, the weight of expectations on African American leaders can be enormous. These expectations, carried by other black employees or by their community, can be a help, but they can also be an enormous burden or source of stress.

The expectations can be helpful because they encourage African Americans to set high standards for themselves, knowing what is expected of them. However, such duties can also be onerous. Rita Farax said that the black community had a valid expectation that she and other blacks would do more than their white counterparts to initiate and support diversity and other people-oriented initiatives. She noted though that this takes "a tremendous amount of energy" and that although others may be able to pass up a project and say they'll come back to it she couldn't. "I don't have the luxury of doing that," she said.

Janet Matthews, an administrative nurse in a major hospital, said her frustrations came when she and her black coworkers had differing expectations of her new role. Because Matthews was the first black woman to hold her job, other blacks felt invested in her success as well as her actions. Matthews just wanted to do her job well but instead had to expend a great deal of energy handling others' expectations. This difference in job expectations caused tensions between Matthews and the other black employees, who might otherwise have been a support base for her.

The overwhelming affirmative response to our survey question regarding blacks' sense of responsibility for helping other African Americans is a testament to blacks' commitment to one another (see Figure 3.1). It is largely due to this joint sense of commitment that so many blacks feel their future success is dependent on what other African Americans do and that they can become elated, depressed, or embarrassed about the words or actions of a black public figure. When Tiger Woods won his first golf tournament, for instance, the black community was elated. However, blacks then felt he repudiated their community by saying he didn't see himself as being just black, and the community felt embarrassed and hurt. Clearly Woods didn't intend to deny his blackness; he intended only to expand his identity to include other aspects of his heritage. This is, however, a perfect example of how the African American community can place additional expectations and burdens on those it considers its members. Other public figures who have gone through similar scrutiny include Colin Powell and Condoleezza Rice.

FIGURE 3.1. Responsibility and African Americans.

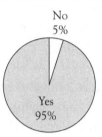

The vast majority of African American leaders say they feel responsible for helping other blacks in the organization.

No
5%

Yes
95%

As a result of feeling personally and collectively invested in the performance and success of black colleagues, blacks maintain a hyperawareness about what fellow African Americans are doing in the organization. It is not unusual for black employees to keep a headcount of how many African Americans work for the organization, what their general roles are, who is in management, how long they've been there, and what power or influence they have. The grapevine buzzes each time another black person is hired. It fairly sings when something happens to one of the company's black managers, good or bad. Additionally, once an African American is hired, other blacks on staff usually begin assessing the new hire on job competence and his or her perceived attitude about being black, asking, in effect: Is this person "black" by my standards? Do we share viewpoints and backgrounds? Is this person likely to help or hinder me and other African Americans here?

What You as African Americans Can Do

The issues and assumptions of responsibility outlined in this chapter are not set in stone. They are the reality that exists, not the reality that *has* to exist. The years we have spent talking with management professionals, black and white, and observing black managers both in a program setting and through their anecdotes, have yielded a set of suggestions for negotiating the gaps between real and perceived commitments. These suggestions include those that are both organizationally and personally focused.

Understanding the organizational context is important as African Americans strive to master the workplace and still be true to themselves. As you work to control the expectations that surround you, you will have to consider how best to communicate, to create an atmosphere of equality, and to set boundaries for yourself with the organization and with other African Americans. Not all the expectations surrounding responsibility are due to organizational factors, though. You also need to recognize and change specific behaviors that allow others—and sometimes even yourself—to create false expectations about your duties.

Communicate your rationale. Organizationally, African Americans can communicate the rationale for their behaviors and decisions to help defray misperceptions. People in the company may confuse African Americans' attempts to network with each other as separatism or any number of negative motivations. For instance, if you as a black leader are asked about the time you are spending with a new black employee, you might say, "If I don't get him acclimated, who will?" By being clear and nondefensive about your rationale and actions, you may lessen the potential for conflict or misunderstanding concerning your behaviors.

Set equal standards. It should be clear to all involved that assisting people with understanding the culture is not the same as favoritism. As managers, African Americans should set equal standards and

---

What African Americans Can Do About Responsibility

Communicate your rationale.

Set equal standards.

Seek out and reward excellence.

Don't overcompensate for other blacks.

Don't let the organization's expectations overwhelm you.

Don't set yourself up as the representative for your race.

Be aware of your own expectations and assumptions.

Be aware of others' expectations.

Take responsibility for your own actions.

Do give back.

---

make sure that all their direct reports follow these standards and are judged by them. As a leader, make sure you clearly and publicly state to your department your expectations and the criteria for evaluations. Also clearly state everyone's goals. Use a variety of media, such as e-mail, your intranet, presentations, and meetings, to reinforce the message. Restate your standards periodically, and make sure you live by them yourself.

Seek out and reward excellence. Managers should look for excellence in all their employees and should reward it equally. Black managers have to guard against rewarding other blacks too easily or not rewarding them at all. A lot of times African Americans, concerned about what their white counterparts will say, treat black colleagues unfairly and even harshly, fearing that otherwise they will be seen as too lenient. In matters of rewards and standards, just strive to be a good manager.

Don't overcompensate for other blacks. Feeling that you bear a responsibility for the welfare of other blacks does not require overcompensating for people who are not performing. Covering up for poor performance does no one any good—not you, the company, the employee, or the race. Remember, the relationship must be two-way. You may be trying to do your best for the other person, but that person also has to be giving you her best effort.

Don't let the organization's expectations overwhelm you. At some point you have to learn to bargain or to say no. Don't let your activities be driven by the organization's expectations. You have got to be your own advocate. Although you can certainly take on extra responsibilities if you desire, find ways to get credit for them. Learn to reprioritize your current responsibilities in the light of the new ones. Negotiate longer timelines on existing projects if new projects are being added to your workload. Tell people you would gladly take on this new project if they could help you determine which of your existing projects should be taken off your plate. Work additional duties into the list of responsibilities on which your performance is evaluated. If you're already doing it, get credit for it.

Don't set yourself up as the representative for your race. You are African American and proud of it; nevertheless, don't set yourself up as the voice of Black America and don't let others do that to you. First, face it, you're not the voice of Black America. Black America has no single voice. Second, although you are an African American and that's an important part of your personality, you are more than that. By allowing yourself to be reduced to only one aspect, you limit yourself and restrict your options. People need to recognize you for more than your blackness. Find ways to expand others' view of you. Get engaged in activities in the company that go beyond racial overtones. Come forward with your hobbies and interests unrelated to race. What you are putting out there is what others will begin to see.

Be aware of your own expectations and assumptions. All black folks aren't out to befriend or support you. In fact some blacks will see you as competition. Additionally, not all African Americans see issues the way that you do, nor should they have to. And just because a person doesn't agree with you on politics, music, or other matters, that doesn't mean they cannot be trusted or that they are not "black." So, get to know people and be open to a good relationship, but don't expect it or assume it solely because of race. In the same vein, all whites are not out to get you either. Some will see you as an ally, and some will share the same interests you have, in and out of the workplace. There are many things on which you can base relationships, so don't limit them.

Be aware of others' expectations. Be aware that many people feel they have the right to tell you what to do and when and where to do it. Actually, they don't. You should commit to those issues and activities that you desire or deem appropriate. It is okay to say no. Identify what is important to you and feasible for you, and act on that information. Do not let responsibility become a burden. Frankly, stressed out, overstretched people who are acting out of duty and not passion are rarely good for anybody. You may choose to do less but to do it better.

Take responsibility for your own actions. Other blacks do not owe you anything. You need to take responsibility for your own actions and for your strengths and developmental needs. Although African Americans and others in general may be good for support or helping you to see where you need assistance, only you can be proactive on your own behalf. Sometimes this means owning up to your own stuff—good and bad. Likewise, sometimes you must let people sink or swim on their own. Although you may go to great lengths to help them, ultimately they have the responsibility for and make the choice about their own actions.

Do give back. Eileen Bender speaks for many when she says, "I feel really compelled to fulfill the biblical principle 'To whom much has been given . . .' There have been so many people who have helped me, I feel compelled to give back, to help in any way I can." We agree, and ask that you do give back. However, give back in the way that is personally and professionally feasible for you. For some individuals this may mean helping people in the family. For others it may mean working in larger community efforts. At the end of the day, if we don't give back, who will?

What You as Colleagues Can Do

It is important that as a non-black, you realize that you too need to moderate your behaviors, expectations, and assumptions about the black sense of responsibility. Because blacks are often responding to what they perceive to be inequities in the corporate system, non-blacks may need to challenge their assumption that all is fair in the workplace. One place to begin challenging this belief about workplace equity is in your personal dealings with black coworkers. This is the first arena in which you can push to see how similar or dissimilar your perceptions are. It is the arena in which you have the greatest ability to work in tandem with African American managers to see that the reality of responsibility becomes more closely aligned with the assumption of equity.

Ensure equitable compensation and opportunities. In dealing with African Americans, or anyone else, be fair with opportunities and compensation. These are times when you won't be able to just go with your gut instincts. Instead, look at records; see whether there are patterns of some groups' getting different kinds of opportunities than others get. Look behind those numbers for the reasons why such disparities exist. Do not allow yourself to rationalize away the differences you may uncover.

Involve black managers. Make sure that African American managers are being involved on an equal basis with other managers. Areas to examine for equal involvement are participation in both formal and informal conversations, assignment to desirable projects, and visibility to executives and the rest of the company. It is impor-

---

What Colleagues Can Do About Responsibility

Ensure equitable compensation and opportunities.

Involve black managers.

Set equal standards.

Give the same benefit of the doubt to all.

Be aware of, not afraid of, affiliations.

Give equal respect.

---

tant that blacks be fully involved as equal partners and team members not only by you but by others as well. As a leader and manager, set a standard of zero tolerance for behaviors that reduce the participation or influence of any member on your team.

Set equal standards. Again, make sure that equal standards are being set for all employees. Like other areas in which equity is crucial, this is something that may need to be carefully checked. Initially, most managers will say they set equal standards for everyone; however, they may not realize that they are asking more or less of their black employees. Their intentions may be different from their actions. Thus, on the one hand, a manager may ask a black direct report or colleague to be on numerous committees without taking into account the time and effort these activities may cost. On the other hand, a manager may make assumptions that a black direct report is not ready for a new task even though he has met the requirements for the job.

Give the same benefit of the doubt to all. Be careful of the ways stereotypes can skew your thinking. Many times African Americans are not given the benefit of the doubt because people unconsciously believe such notions as "they don't want to work"; "they don't understand"; "they're prone to being emotional." Although people may not always think these thoughts consciously, even unarticulated thoughts may guide one's actions. In *The Fifth Discipline Fieldbook*, Peter Senge and his colleagues discuss the mental models people hold and how these models affect individuals' behaviors. According to Senge, these models, these unconscious assumptions that we all have, may direct our behavior more strongly than we realize. To begin to discern what mental models you have about other people and how these models may affect you, honestly monitor your responses to and thoughts about whites and blacks who are in similar situations. If you find that you tend to think a little differently about a group or person within a group, begin to delve into the reasons why. The point of this activity is not to suggest that everyone is a racist but that many people are driven by beliefs that are so ingrained they are not aware that these beliefs exist. Consequently, the only way to determine whether they exist is to honestly and consciously look for them.

Be aware of, not afraid of, affiliations. This idea goes hand-in-hand with the understanding that acknowledging difference is the first step on the path to understanding and finding strength in difference. Recognize that the identification of African Americans and other people of difference with each other is not a threat to you personally or to your group. Their affiliation is a source of strength and support. Appreciate the affiliations others may have as a positive means through which they express their identity, provide service to others, and potentially, grow as leaders.

Give equal respect. Beneath all successful corporate relationships lies respect. Giving respect is as much a reflection on the people you give respect to as it is on yourself. Respect comes out not only in your interactions with individuals but in larger group dynamics. By demonstrating respect for individuals equally, both professionally and personally, you can help to create an environment in which being different is more of a fact and less of a burden. By respecting others, you can encourage their trust in you as a leader and open the door to deeper, more rewarding relationships, the relationships through which much of an organization's business gets done.

———————

Although many blacks recognize their shared responsibility to each other, they also understand that as men and women they are having very different workplace experiences. The stereotypes associated with gender combine with the issues associated with race to create very different challenges for black men and black women. As we discuss in the next chapter, the dynamics that can result affect everything from compensation and job assignments to specific interpersonal interactions.

4

Navigating the Shoals of Race and Gender

A hush fell over the room as one by one, nine out of the ten men raised their hands. The moment was both ludicrous and incredibly real as the men, all of whom were African American and participants in the Center for Creative Leadership's African-American Leadership Program, admitted that they gave job appraisals to their white, female direct reports only with the door ajar. They said they weren't willing to take any chances their behaviors would be misread— either by the women or by others passing the office. As black men they had to be cautious, they said, when dealing with white women.

We have found this phenomenon to be a common one. Although other black men may not feel that they have to leave the door open when they are having private conversations with white women, many black men do think that the beliefs surrounding black men and white women are problematic and stereotypical. One of the stereotypes that haunts African American leaders is the perception of black men as sexual predators. Johnson McDaniel, a manager at a major chemical company, says one of the burdens that a black man carries is the perception that "I'm a black male, and gee whiz, I love every white woman."

The issue of race and the issue of gender can be challenging when each is regarded separately; taken together they become even more complex. When race and gender combine, the issues surrounding each subgroup multiply. Women are not just women, for example, they are *white* women, *black* women, *Asian* women, and so forth; each combination tends to evoke different connotations in the corporate setting and elicit a different reaction from others. The same holds true for men, and black men in particular. As a result, the issues surrounding someone perceived as a black male are more complicated than those surrounding someone perceived just as being black, and they are different from those surrounding someone perceived just as being male.

This chapter explores the quality of the miasma that looms at the crossroads of race and gender and the associated consequences for black men and women. It may appear a bit different from the other chapters in this book. Like the others it examines how race and another element combine to create unique nuances for blacks in corporate America. Unlike the others, however, it looks at not one but two characteristics over which individuals have no control, and each of which holds its own position in the current hierarchy of status and influence. In this examination, race and gender can be clearly compared against the white male norm. It is a commonly known fact that in terms of pay, prestige, and opportunity, white males set the standard. Numerous studies since the mid-1990s have emphasized how certain nontraditional groups compare with white men in these areas. Although these reports often reflect the differences between white males and other groups in stark numbers, they rarely explore the quality or impact of these differences in terms of the experiences of these other groups. However, that information is critically important in understanding how and why different groups may interpret their experiences differently, and differently from the experiences of white men in particular.

There is yet another variable that makes the arena of race combined with gender unique. Throughout this book, we argue that there is no singular, monolithic black experience. In spotlighting gender, we hope to firmly shatter the notion that all blacks are living the same lives. Indeed, African American men and women are having very different experiences in the workplace in many respects, both in how others perceive them and in how they themselves view their professional experiences. Although they are both black, they are also both *gendered*. When African Americans are dealing with people who are not black, this double identity can create interesting challenges and opportunities. And when dealing with each other, black men and women may be more likely to experience or notice purely gender issues, because they tend to hold race as a constant when dealing with one another.

What the Combination of Race and Gender Looks Like

Gender, race, and the combination thereof can affect the degree to which an individual is given responsibilities and opportunities in the workplace. Common areas in which inequalities appear are salary; access to important, or "visible," projects and people; promotions; and explicit and implicit job responsibilities. Less obvious but still dynamic are the tensions that arise from the expectations and perceptions that tend to accompany each combination of race and gender. All these can be fed, for better or worse, by stereotypes.

Stereotypes

For both men and women in general, stereotypes abound, and many people play into them. These stereotypes can enhance or limit people's perceptions of others' ability. They can also affect the expectations placed on individuals, particularly those making their way in corporate America. For example, men are stereotypically expected to be self-confident, independent, and in control of their emotions. They are also more likely than women to be assumed to be leaders, or to have leadership potential, and are generally perceived to be more competent than their female counterparts. However, men also contend with the stereotype of the sexual predator, as some people worry that men view the workplace as a pickup ground. Additionally, men who are quick to express emotions and those perceived as insecure or incompetent may stand out as contrary to the norm.

Although black men may benefit from some of the stereotypes about males, they may also lose ground in the eyes of their white colleagues owing to stereotypes about blacks. Consequently, in addition to being viewed as independent and in control of their emotions, black men are often stereotyped as sexually predatory, athletic, threatening, intimidating, or angry. In talking about these stereotypes, McDaniel says that in his opinion, people believe that all black men want white women: "You know, it's another one of these unwritten rules. Two things you don't mess with in this corporation are the corporation's women and the corporation's money." He also adds, "all of us don't have guns, knives, and we don't all use dope. . . . And incidentally, all of us are supposed to be an authority on sports, particularly basketball, football, and baseball." Other black men say they have to be especially careful if they are large, particularly if they are large and dark complexioned. Henry Wate, also a manager at a chemical company and a self-described "fairly big-framed black man," laments that he has to pay special attention to his acts, behaviors, and mannerisms. "I have to be cognizant in what I do so that I'm not viewed as being intimidating." James Kelley agrees: "I have to be very careful about body language and choice of words in dealing with some people. Part of this is because I'm on the larger side. I can be intimidating just by being a black male and large." For black men, the consequences of being stereotyped can be severe. Images of them as being angry, sexual predators, not quite as competent as white males, and intimidating can hamper their progress in corporate America by unfairly assigning to them behaviors or intentions that are in no way representative of them individually. Such stereotypes also contribute to black managers' perception that they have to work twice as hard in the workplace.

Women in general face their own set of stereotypes. They tend to be portrayed as supportive, cooperative, nurturing, overly emotional, and as sexual objects. They are also typically seen as less competent than their male counterparts, often because they are believed to be less committed to their jobs and because they are said to be lacking in experience. Additionally, women are often maligned or even penalized for pushing their behavior beyond boundaries others have set. A recent CCL study asked women leaders about the values that men and women were rewarded for in their corporations. Respondents said men were typically rewarded for being assertive and impartial whereas women were rewarded for displaying less dominant qualities. It stands to reason, then, that women who regularly display those qualities for which men are normally rewarded may find themselves punished for acting counter to expected or desired norms. This also hampers some women's progress, as dominant behaviors are the ones generally rewarded in the workplace and are often required for success.

Like their male counterparts, African American women deal with stereotypes that are largely negative. They are often considered too aggressive, too direct, too assertive, and too "flashy" for mainstream corporate America. This particular set of stereotypes appears to have grown from cultural behaviors of African American women that confuse their colleagues. Ironically, numerous studies that examine the behaviors of black women suggest they are socialized to be assertive, independent, and self-confident—behaviors more often associated with white men than with women of any color. In CCL's African-American Leadership Program, black women regularly report that they are perceived as being too direct and aggressive. One chemical corporation manager we interviewed, Jan Henry, told us, "As a black woman I tend to be very, very direct about how I understand things or questions that I ask." She went on to say that there are about fifteen other black professional women in her organization, all of whom have very different personalities and different work styles, and yet at some point in their careers all of them have been told they are "too direct."

Often, being direct and other traits that are considered positive in a man are seen as negative when expressed by a woman, particularly a black one. Another black woman, Angel Smith, a manager in a consulting firm, told us of a conversation she had with an African American male colleague concerning how the other men at work, most of whom were white, viewed her. Judging from their conversations with the black male colleague, these men saw Smith as attractive, intelligent, and direct. And, he concluded, they were afraid of her, because she might be seen as competition for them. "And if I had all the same characteristics that I have now and I were white?" she asked. "I think they would find you intriguing," he answered, "because they might see you as being more acceptable." As this story illustrates, black women, who tend to take a little from Column A and a little from Column B in terms of stereotypical male and female behaviors, can find themselves between a rock and a hard place. Instead of being viewed as strong and independent, black women are often stereotyped as aggressive, emasculating, or unfeminine.

Tension

Although men and women work together daily in the corporate world, they do not do so without some sources of tension. People may experience tension in the workplace because of the stereotypes and equity issues previously mentioned. Tensions may also revolve around the kind of visibility one gets and whether one receives high-profile or challenging assignments. Here, as in other situations, there are perceived gender implications. A recent CCL study examining corporate leaders' experience suggests that women leaders receive fewer high-profile or developmental assignments than their male counterparts. The implications of this assignment pattern are far-reaching because these assignments not only give people critical visibility, they also help managers learn and hone skills that will make them better leaders in the future. Not surprisingly, women who are stereotyped as being too emotional and less experienced than men are often not seen as being competent or ready to be full and equal partners. Such stereotypes add to the tension women experience in the workplace.

For African Americans, additional issues can aggravate these tensions. For example, some black men feel they are being disrespected because they are not receiving the full measure of benefits of being male in the workplace. Although they have the same gender as their white male colleagues, they know their maleness does not result in equal pay or status. "White males don't give you the respect you deserve," says Bill Wilton, an associate manager at an insurance company. "You have education in one area and they put you somewhere else to work that's not even related. . . . They don't respect anything about you." Black men also have tensions around their relationships with white women. As stated earlier, many are concerned that their relationships with white women will be misread. Beyond that, many also feel white women are surpassing them in the workplace, producing yet another slight to their masculinity.

Black women often feel hard-pressed by workplace tensions as well. Among the biggest sources of tension are their white female counterparts. In many instances, white women feel they can and should make common cause with black women—as sisters in arms on the male-dominated corporate battlefield. Some black women, however, feel differently. "You're going to face some of the same stereotypes," argues Monica Stewart, a team leader for a medical research organization, discussing the common struggles of black and white women, "but you still have different issues because [white women] don't have that 'double whammy.'" Female participants in The African-American Leadership Program often agreed, saying they believe white women do not value black women's issues and concerns and are apt to prioritize women's issues around white women's concerns.

How African American women and white men get along is yet another issue and oftentimes a question. Many black women believe that white men want to distance themselves from them. Others believe white men are willing to work more closely with them than with either black men or white women. "One of the things I found out," says chemical company program manager Helen Thompson, "is that white men in the company are very unsure about black women and their ability. They are also uncomfortable, and I have had many discussions with them around this issue." Larry Wiggins, a human resource manager, disagrees, saying that in his experience, minority women who have been successful in getting mentors have mentors who are white men. African American men, he said, do not get the same benefit.

The answer to the question of who can get closer to the wielders of power—usually white men—is critical for African Americans assessing their chances for moving up, fully contributing, and succeeding in corporate America. Anecdotal evidence suggests some blacks believe African American women can get closer to white men because they tend to be direct in their communications; they can be spoken to as if they were men, without the threat of competition because they are not men. Conversely, separate studies by David Thomas of Harvard University and the Center for Creative Leadership suggest that black women are the least likely to get mentored. Thomas speculates that black women receive less mentoring because they have less in common with white men than either black men or white women do and thus less common ground on which to build mentoring relationships. In Chapter Six, we discuss the differences in mentoring in greater depth and detail. Whatever the exact statistics, these issues around access and mentoring contribute to the tensions permeating the corporate environment.

Why Race and Gender Are Important

Because race and gender are unchangeable aspects of one's identity, their impact on work experiences depends to a great degree on the perceptions and reactions of others. Race and gender—individually and combined—are laden with preconceptions. They affect African Americans' opportunities to develop strong corporate relationships and to receive equity in the workplace.

Trust and Respect

Trust and respect are the foundation for developing and maintaining successful corporate relationships. As mentioned earlier, it is through these relationships that much of an organization's business gets done. If trust and respect are undermined or unduly influenced by the racial and gender stereotypes that people carry, then those in power are much less likely to believe in the abilities of or give opportunities to those who are different from themselves. Lack of trust can keep African American men and women from granting or capitalizing on opportunities and creating alliances. Such attitudes are certainly evident in many of the leaders we have surveyed. As Jan Henry says, "Black women need to be aware that white women are different, and white men are by and large not comfortable with us."

Perceptions

Learning how race and gender combine to affect interpersonal relations can help individuals understand how their own beliefs may be getting in the way of their ability to effectively carry out their leadership responsibilities. For a white male manager to understand, for instance, that he believes that black men are particularly dangerous or that black women must be watched with a wary eye can start that manager on the road to creating a more impartial work environment. The awareness enables him to make more educated decisions, taking into account the ways individual biases and beliefs might be influencing his decision-making process.

An understanding of the ways race and gender can combine to create specific attitudes helps you avoid being limited by those attitudes. Although this understanding may not shield you from the effects of others' biases, it *can* keep you from internalizing those beliefs and allowing them to damage your belief in yourself.

Equity

Multiple studies by researchers make it clear that gender affects pay and status in the workplace. Catalyst, an organization that studies corporate women, revealed in a 1997 study that women in all racial groups earn less than men in those same groups (see Figure 4.1). In his book *Race, Gender and Rhetoric,* John Fernandez reports that women constitute half the workforce, but are less than one-half of 1 percent of the highest-paid officers and directors of the top 1,000 U.S. companies. Women hold only 2.6 percent of the top executive positions at Fortune 500 companies. In addition, Fernandez says, female managers work about 52.5 hours a week and men work about 52 hours, yet men make an average of $55,000 a year and women earn about $44,000.

FIGURE 4.1. Pay Comparison, by Race and Gender.

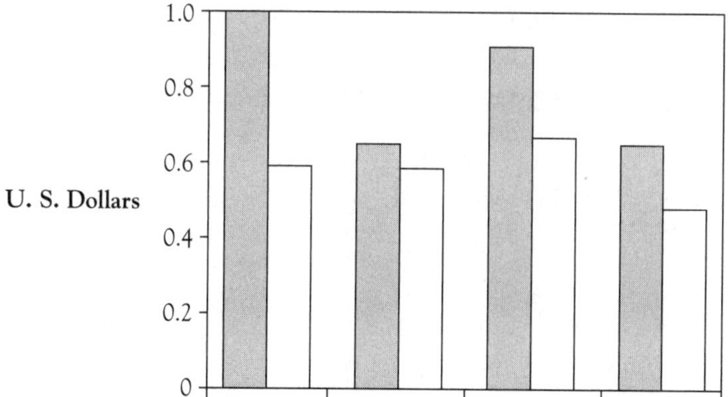

	White	Black	Asian	Latino
◼ Men	$1.00	$0.65	$0.91	$0.65
☐ Women	$0.59	$0.58	$0.67	$0.48

Source: Adapted from Catalyst, *Women of Color in Corporate Management,* 1997.

When race and gender are combined, these equity issues take on a slightly different flavor. According to the Catalyst study summarized in Figure 4.1, black and Latino male managers make about $0.65 for every $1.00 that white male managers make, and Asian male managers make $0.91. Black women managers earn only $0.58 for every $1.00 that white male managers earn, whereas white women managers earn about $0.59, Asian women managers $0.67, and Latino women managers $0.48. These findings suggest that African American men, like men in other ethnic groups, receive a benefit for being male. Although this benefit translates into pay and status advances over black, white, and Latinas (although not Asian women), it does not amount to nearly the benefit that men who are white receive. And though black women make almost as much money as do white women, Fernandez notes that they are also more likely than their white peers to have advanced degrees. Thus, despite having more academic preparation, they earn a little less money.

What does all this imply? That race and gender make a potent combination, with significant effects on workplace equity.

What Is Unique to the Black Experience

The road to leadership for African American men and women is not the same, but the issues each gender faces are related. The dynamics of gender play out in the amounts and types of leadership opportunity available for black professionals. These dynamics add to the list of workplace stresses and pressures that spring from being different. They also mean that African Americans, especially women, often must deal with the questions of whether their successes (or the roadblocks they face) are related to their own achievements or to gender or race factors.

African American Men Versus African American Women

One of the big arguments in the African American corporate community is over who is doing "better" or "worse" at work, black men or black women. Not only do black men and women disagree on the answer, but black women themselves disagree. Many take the side of their brothers when they discuss what is happening in corporate America. On the one hand, Jan Henry says that as she looked at corporate America, she found white men at the top, then white females, then black males, and then black females. HR director Rita Farax agrees: "Black women in the corporation, in my opinion, have the most difficult time moving up, being visible, getting opportunities. It's a much tougher role, even when you compare it down to black men." On the other hand, Bill Wilton says, "I think the person that's on the bottom of the totem pole, as far as getting promoted, is the black male. I think the white female is next and then the black female is above that." Black men and women often interpret this tension as competition between each other.

Not all black women agree with Henry and Farax. Marcella Watkins offers an interesting twist on the debate between black men and women. "White men see me as a sexual being," she says, "there's allure. They want you to be around. You don't get opportunities, but you get a curiosity, to find out a little bit more about [you]. . . . Once I get a window open, I can make do. Let me show you what I can do. Black men don't get that opening." Candice Casey, now a team leader in a national financial company, reports that in most of the industries in which she has worked, African American women were forgiven their mistakes more easily than were African American men. "It just seems like the black male, especially, needs to get it right the first time," she says.

As with the argument about black women and their acceptability to white men, anecdotal evidence weighs heavily on both sides. Examining the statistics illuminates where and why some of the confusion arises. Census figures taken in 2000 suggest that there are about 800,000 more managerial and professional black women in the workforce than there are black men. However, salary information (discussed earlier in the chapter) reveals that although there may be fewer African American men than women at the managerial level, the men are being better paid. That blacks disagree about who receives better treatment suggests that both men and women are struggling and are therefore sensitive to any opportunities others get and to any slights they perceive.

It's Just One More Thing

The stress arising from the combination of race and gender is just one more factor contributing to the overall pressure of existing in the business environment. Figure 4.2 is but one illustration of the differences many African Americans experience. Although more black men than women in our study believed they understand and ably handle the politics of their workplace environments, black women were more likely than black men to think it is important to engage or actively participate in these activities to be accepted or to get ahead. "Being a black woman puts on a lot more pressure," says Gayle Harris, a corporate training analyst. "You've got to deal with white females, black males, and black females." Deborah Raleigh, a vice president at a major manufacturing conglomerate, says she has to question how much of her success is her own and how much can be attributed to her race and gender. "I would like to think my performance plays a larger role than my race and gender. But I don't know that for a fact, and I don't think I will ever know that."

What You as African Americans Can Do

The most effective strategies for dealing with the double-whammy that being black and gendered can mean to your workplace experience focus on cultivating interpersonal strengths and understanding interpersonal dynamics. By developing your ability to form deeper workplace relationships, you can move beyond the stereotypes that may affect others' perceptions. You can also develop an infrastructure that will support you when issues of stereotyping arise.

FIGURE 4.2. Office Politics and African American Men and Women.

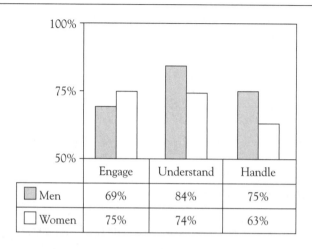

	Engage	Understand	Handle
☐ Men	69%	84%	75%
☐ Women	75%	74%	63%

Cultivate your trust. Do things that establish and build trust between and among groups—whether racial, gender, or both. This includes establishing open and honest dialogue with others, respecting each other's private areas, and offering the benefit of the doubt. We admit, though, that this dialogue has to be seasoned with wisdom. Fear, or the lack of being in a safe haven, has been one of the reasons African Americans are reticent to share their private world. In many cases they have feared exposing their vulnerabilities to others, and in some cases they have been justified in their fear. We believe that leaders have to have trusting relationships with others. But we also believe that to create deeply trusting relationships, people need to go slowly, respecting each other's private areas until each person involved is willing to open them. An important component of building trust is being willing to give others the benefit of the doubt. In our interviews, we often heard people who were quite willing to believe or assume the worst about white women or white men. We suggest, instead, that you be willing to trust or to believe that which is positive until you are proved wrong. This difference in viewpoint is crucial because it can affect how you interpret people's behaviors and thus how you respond to them.

What African Americans Can Do About Race and Gender

Cultivate your trust.

Demand equitable treatment and enforce it for others.

Create alliances.

Understand how your behaviors are perceived.

Find trusted agents.

Demand equitable treatment and enforce it for others. We suggest that you look at the work patterns in your department and notice whether any particular group, in this case any racial or gender group, is being treated in a systematically different way from the majority group. For example, are qualified black people being overlooked for particular assignments in favor of those less qualified? Are female peers consistently asked to take notes at meetings when administrative assistants are not present? If this is the case, stand up for yourself and others and demand equitable treatment. Although demanding your rights is not synonymous with being uncivil, it does mean being willing to vigorously and compellingly stand up for yourself. By the same token you should be willing to enforce equitable treatment for others as well. If the workplace is to be equitable, it cannot be so for blacks only. You need to be willing to see injustice as it occurs for all groups, not just your own.

Create alliances. Find common cause with other groups. It is easiest to start with groups with whom you already have something in common, such as gender groups, ethnic minority groups, or other groups of disempowered people in the organization. Creating alliances is about forging support with groups with the goal of making all participants stronger. In order to do this, however, you have to be able to see beyond the confines of your particular group's issues and see how those issues fit into the larger system. Additionally, there may be wisdom in creating or solidifying alliances with those already in positions of power. Partner with those in a position to provide an opportunity to showcase talent, to supply valuable feedback about performance, and to offer insight into developmental opportunities.

Understand how your behaviors are perceived. It is important to understand how your behaviors may be perceived in your organization so that you can work proactively to manage perceptions and understand and evaluate the consequences of your actions. An example of such an understanding might be the decision by some black men to close their doors but open their internal office blinds (if available) when they provide women with performance appraisals. In this instance these men are attempting to manage the impression others may have about their motives and behaviors. Although you may not be able to manage every perception, by understanding how others interpret particular behaviors, you have the opportunity to anticipate the consequences and determine whether you are willing to take them. Thus your risks become more deliberate, measured, and planned, and the results of these actions don't come as a surprise.

Find trusted agents. Find people you trust in the dominant groups (race or gender) and periodically check in with them about your issues, behaviors, and perceptions. It is often difficult to know or understand how others may interpret your behaviors. However, if you have one or more people you can trust in those other groups, they may be able to help you see how people like themselves may perceive and interpret your behaviors. Be willing to reciprocate the effort of your trusted agents by serving in a similar capacity for them and becoming a part of their learning experience as well. Diverse groups often don't know a lot about one another. So if blacks are to move beyond mere superficialities in their interpersonal relationships, they have to be willing to educate and to be educated by and about others—even around some of the *tough* issues.

What You as Colleagues Can Do

Because race and gender are two fundamental aspects that none of us can change, the key to clearing the miasma that surrounds these aspects is to adjust the way we view, or don't view, them. As a colleague of African American men and women, you can do this by consciously developing an open mind-set and proactively soliciting relationships that cross race and gender lines. In developing cross-race and cross-gender relationships, it is vital to maintain your awareness of difference without letting that difference be intimidating or divisive.

Recognize that relationships are a two-way street. To improve relationships between groups, people have to be willing to initiate and participate in *real* conversations. They must actively do things that continuously build trust, including opening doors for formal and informal dialogue. These types of conversations are often left for disempowered groups to start, but if that is what you are waiting for, the conversation may never begin. Many African Americans believe the cost may be too high if they try to start a conversation about race with a partner who is not ready. The cost, in this case, might be getting labeled as "radical" or "militant" or "someone who sees race in everything." These labels, many blacks may fear, can take on a life of their own and destroy the individual's chances for upward mobility in the organization. Introducing such conversations is less risky for the groups with a power advantage—so you may need to take the first step.

Respect all people. Although the idea of respecting people regardless of race and gender may seem Pollyannaishly simple, it is actually fairly difficult to put into practice. To accomplish this goal effectively, look closely at your attitudes for any conscious—and perhaps more important, unconscious—biases that may be driving your thought processes and behaviors. Sometimes you may not be able to complete this process without receiving input from an out-

---

What Colleagues Can Do About Race and Gender

Recognize that relationships are a two-way street.

Respect all people.

Don't overassume similarities.

Find trusted agents.

---

side source; a trusted agent from a minority group can help you see your behaviors more clearly. As a part of this process, people have to recognize what stereotypes they may have accepted as true or partially true, and then work to free themselves of these influences. People need to recognize the uniqueness of each individual and at the same time recognize the impact of ethnic and other group identities. Work to promote respectful individual and systemic treatment for all in your organization. Depending on your corporate responsibilities, you might do this through policymaking, hiring and promotional practices, assignment of projects, and so forth.

Don't overassume similarities. Don't overassume similarities between your experiences and those of people of different groups. Oftentimes such an assumption can feel condescending or overly pushy to those in the other groups. Although there are always some similarities, assuming more similarities than exist can work to separate, to add to the alienation, rather than to bring you and others closer together. One classic example involves the relationship between black and white women. As mentioned previously in this chapter, many white women have erroneously assumed a familiarity with black women that black women don't always feel and sometimes resent. Having something like race or gender in common certainly can be a starting place for developing a bond, but the relationship must be nurtured as the differences between the groups are acknowledged, respected, and understood in terms of both challenges and opportunities.

Find trusted agents. We believe that you should find trusted agents among your black colleagues for the same reasons we suggest African Americans should do so among those who are not black. Keep in mind, though, that your agent can speak only for himself or herself, not for African Americans at large. In fact it is reasonable to assume that if you view your agent as a group spokesperson, she most likely will not see you as a trustworthy agent. Built into this notion of establishing or maintaining a relationship with a trusted agent is the idea that you and your agent recognize each other as individuals who may be able to shed light on a group's behavior rather than as people who are indistinguishable from the group. Finally, please be aware that if you haven't successfully done so already, building a meaningful relationship with a trusted black agent may require time and energy. One reason for this is African Americans' fear of being labeled a "house Negro." During the era of slavery in this country, those who lived or worked in the master's quarters were often perceived by other blacks as having greater access and opportunities than those who tended the fields and who therefore did not have a "realistic" experience. This perception has carried forward in some ways to the corporate setting, where those who are closer to or part of the inner circle of power may be perceived as untrustworthy by their black colleagues who do not have the same access.

The organizational and relationship dynamics that stem from the combination of identity, responsibility, and gender are complex. Understanding their interplay and the nuances of their expression sets the groundwork for understanding and building purposeful professional relationships. In the next chapter, we explore how African Americans network and how they can use networking effectively for personal and professional benefit.

5

Working the Networks

Keith Shields, a senior vice president of a national financial institution, laughed as he walked and talked with his colleagues. As they made their way across the golf course, Shields carefully noted his coworkers' backswings, how they handled bungled shots, and of course, the information they were sharing. As the person who voluntarily took responsibility for the beer cart, Shields was in the thick of things—which was exactly where he wanted to be.

"I don't golf," Shields says; "my skills weren't good enough to be competitive." Yet he realized that by not golfing he might hurt or at least limit his chances of moving up in the corporation, because others "had this common sport to use as a framework. It was very evident that the bank executive culture was a golf culture, and they played [golf] well." By not playing golf, Shields was limiting his exposure to the higher-level executives who routinely played the game. People who were on the golf course gained additional face time with these executives, and the executives got to know them better. As Shields explains, "I'm not going to get to know you in a forty-five-minute interview, but golf, even eight holes, takes several hours, and I can see how you work under adversity."

It was after recognizing how much he was missing that Shields, a former assistant secretary to a high-ranking political appointee in the Clinton administration, decided he would tend the beer cart.

"You just find a way to not get pushed out. In executive ranks it's not so much mental, it's how you get along."

For many African American leaders the thought of tending the beer cart or taking similar actions feels too close to subservience to be comfortable. However, Shields doesn't see his actions as being subservient at all. Instead, he sees them as tools for developing relations between social equals and business colleagues. "You've got to take that chip off your shoulder," he says. According to Shields, it just made good sense to place himself where the business leaders of his company were going to be. In this way he was part of the conversation, he could be seen, and he could do these things on his own terms. He didn't have to play golf, and, he says, "People got to know who I was."

We offer Keith Shields's story not to suggest how all African Americans should network, but to underscore the importance of networking itself. In addition, Shields's story illustrates how African Americans can stretch their networking comfort zone. By considering how he could be included rather than whether he would be seen as a servant, Shields expanded his networking opportunities and maneuvered his way into the inner circle. By being bound by their own stereotypes or those of others, being unwilling to try something new, or being unwilling to place themselves in a position to hear what's going on in the office, many African Americans contribute to their own exclusion from informational loops. In essence, *not* networking helps to increase invisibility for those who are already vulnerable to being overlooked.

For years, business books and magazine articles have extolled the virtues of networking. They report that networking is relatively simple, beneficial to one's career, and largely up to one's own discretion. Compared to whites' networks, African Americans' networks have been identified as being relatively weak and less productive and expansive. Unfortunately, African Americans usually have not been told why this is so or what they should do about it. For many people in corporate America, networking is the process of creating and maintaining relationships to enhance work opportunities, gather information, and secure social and emotional support. This is certainly true for African Americans too, but we suggest that networking is also something more for African Americans. It is a goal as well as a process, an end as well as a means. It is through networking that blacks find and practice their identity in the corporate world. It is also through networking that they can gather strength to continue working in what is at times a subtly hostile environment. Through networking, many blacks play out their sense of responsibility to each other. And through networking, many share with each other the perils they face in the workplace and possible strategies to avoid or overcome them.

However, although African Americans have many reasons to nurture strong networks, they also have a plethora of reasons for the relative weakness believed to exist in their current networks. The latter include issues of trust and access and differing beliefs about how, why, and with whom it is important to network. Some of these reasons—such as concerns about trust and distrust—are not always easy to see or understand, yet they have an enormous effect on workplace relationships. We believe that owing to miasma, African American networking patterns may be stronger than is believed yet weaker than they appear. This paradox arises from the inability or unwillingness of many in corporate America to see where the actual strengths and weaknesses of African American networking patterns reside.

A recent Center for Creative Leadership study revealed that blacks who network with other blacks in their organization at comparatively high levels are seen as more effective leaders than are those blacks who do not make such strong use of their African American colleagues. This is in spite of the fact that many blacks are directly and indirectly advised to avoid being regularly seen with other African Americans. This advice has come from whites and other blacks, from peers and higher-ups. At the same time, it is much harder for some blacks to develop more than perfunctory relationships with their white colleagues, because they feel the need to always keep up their "game face," rarely letting their true personae show through. Because of this, many whites may think their relationships with their black colleagues are stronger than they actually are. Conversely, whites who have forged true and honest relationships with black colleagues might be surprised at the strength of those bonds. That strength is a result of the effort exerted in creating them.

For all individuals, networking is a personal endeavor. For blacks, networking—like mentoring and taking responsibility for others— can be personal and perilous. Consequently, it is important for all leaders and their organizations to determine what networking looks like and how it differs for African American leaders.

What Networking Looks Like

We define *networking* as creating and maintaining relationships to enhance work opportunities and to secure social and emotional support. Although this definition applies to networking by all professionals, we have found that lack of full trust between blacks and whites in the workplace hampers effective networking for African Americans. As discussed in previous chapters, many blacks perceive that whites may not always honor them as full and equal corporate partners nor grant them full access to opportunities and information. Such behaviors, many blacks feel, create significant barriers to networking. If you are not seen as an equal nor given equal access, how can your networking be as effective or inclusive as the networking of those who are given equal access and opportunity?

Trust

For some blacks in corporate America, the issue is less one of opportunity and more one of trust. They do not trust whites with personal information. Anna Dutch, senior executive of a professional sports team, speaks of the black employees who come to her. "I'm the only person they feel they can talk to. . . . It's the whole thing about trust." On the issue of trusting whites, Maurice Greene, vice president of an international financial company, says, "I hope for the best, but I expect it to be short of the best." Such an attitude, Greene adds, makes you "become a chameleon and learn how to hide what you really feel." Networking relationships are built by establishing personal rapport, which comes from frank exchanges about thoughts and experiences. When such relationships are conducted through the "armor" of protective mechanisms, it is hard to establish deep or intimate connections.

Some distrust comes from experience of interactions between blacks and whites; however, other elements of distrust seem to spring from cultural differences in the ways different groups approach personal information. Thomas Kochman, in *Black and White Styles in Conflict*, argues that as a group, whites are more willing to share personal information than are blacks. This behavioral difference between the two groups has been confirmed on numerous occasions by participants in CCL's African-American Leadership Program. Time and again they have discussed how white colleagues shared more personal information than blacks believed was appropriate. In addition, some have been frustrated to learn that white colleagues have often shared black colleagues' personal information as well, information that the blacks assumed would be kept private. After one participant in the program relates such a story, others will say, "That's why I don't share my personal stuff with them." Someone else may chime in, "Yeah, they'll use it against you."

The consequence of these diverse attitudes to the confidentiality of personal information is that whites and blacks may be looking for different things in a networking relationship, and that difference may cause a friction of misunderstanding that feeds into the feelings of distrust. The result? Blacks often perceive that whites not only share too much of their own personal information but expect blacks to share their personal lives as well—and this is a source of discomfort and awkwardness for blacks. "I wish [my white counterparts] understood that I was caring," says telecommunications company sales manager Eileen Bender, "but we need to maintain a certain level of professionalism. Some colleagues, however, may want to be more personally involved. The weight of this may be more than you can desire or imagine. Recognize that it may not be mutual. I'll share a little, but I'm not about to bring in my dirty laundry." For many blacks the issue of trust revolves around how much they are willing to trust anyone, regardless of race. Keith Shields, who says he gives everyone, black or white, only about 85 percent of his full capacity to trust, also notes, "The most recent people who have disappointed me have been an African American female and an African American male."

Not every African American in the business world distrusts everyone white, or vice versa. Nevertheless distrust in the workplace and the misuse and misinterpretation of shared information has a debilitating impact on networking in general, creating invisible obstacles to the formation of relationships.

Formal Networking

Formal networking typically consists of relationships formed in accordance with organizational necessity. These relationships develop as a result of the workflow or purposeful interactions occurring at the office. People network with clients, superiors, peers, and direct reports because their job mandates that they do so, not necessarily because it is their choice. However, for African Americans, the issue is not only with whom they network, but how they network. Despite the links created as a by-product of the formal networking process, blacks are often faced with the additional challenge of having to manage others' perceptions or misperceptions of their behaviors. Therefore, something that should be an objective, uninhibited process can be stymied by the differences in styles, expectations, and prejudices of blacks and their non-black colleagues.

Informal Networking

Informal networking is the area in which people exercise the most discretion over those with whom they network. Unlike formal networking, which is largely determined by organizational requirements, informal networking consists of interacting with people with whom you choose to spend your time. Some of these relationships are by-products of formal networking, although the deepening of such relationships usually comes about informally. And some come about simply because people have chosen to interact with each other.

In looking at human interaction, social scientists have shown that people tend to form relationships with people who are like themselves. Such relationships are fairly easy to create because people who are like each other often have similar experiences and understandings of events. These connections tend to make communications smoother and behaviors easier to predict, thus making people more comfortable with each other. Studies have also shown that race and gender are two "like" factors around which people are likely to bond. In and of itself, the tendency to be with like others is not a racial or racist behavior. In fact this is a behavior common to most groups. However, because whites are the most powerful and dominant group in the workforce, their desire to be with like others can have a devastating affect on other groups in the workplace. Robert Stanley, a vice president in a major polling firm, believes that he has lost opportunities because of people's desire to be with like others. "Generally people like to be around people who are like them," he says. "They're more comfortable. In the world headquarters [of my company] there are two African Americans on staff. Because some whites might not feel comfortable [with us] . . . information is not shared."

Whether as a byproduct of people's tendency to be with like others or intentional exclusion, many African Americans still find it hard to penetrate the informal groups in their workplace. These groups can range from lunchroom cliques to the regulars who gather for drinks at the local watering hole after work. Rita Farax, HR director at a major chemical company, says that the natural groupings at her organization assist employees in their careers and that African Americans are excluded from those groupings. This exclusion, she says, "prevents you from ever getting in the networks . . . that exist in the company, the powerful networks that you would need to be a part of if you were really going to be as successful as you could be." Though these organizations are not formal, she says, they "are part of the fixtures of the company." Henry Wate, who is also a manager at a chemical company, believes that breaking into the "old boy's network" is key for African Americans. By becoming a part of this network, Wate hopes blacks can attain positions of influence and organizational power "so we can begin to make some inroads and influence into the next wave of what this company is going to be like in terms of how it uses its people."

Robert Stanley notes that people often talk about "the club" in figurative terms, but for some the club is literal. Stanley has a good relationship with his boss, a company vice chairman, but laments that a white male colleague has a much better relationship. "On Fridays I go home. [This colleague] and the vice chairman are playing golf [at the country club]. Because he has access to the vice chairman in an informal setting, he has a different relationship. Information is shared, an understanding of hot buttons is gained. I can't say that the club has a whites-only situation, but most country clubs don't have a lot of black males as members." Stanley's situation is a good example of how the reality of social practice and convention may make it difficult to network, even when the formal rules suggest an openness to networking.

Although African Americans may have difficulty breaking into some white networks, they generally have an easier time breaking into the organization's black networks. Although these might not have the organizational power of some of the more mainstream groups, they can still greatly assist African Americans in their careers. Indeed, the previous chapters on identity and responsibility and the upcoming chapter on mentoring all suggest ways that

African Americans can use networking to help each other negotiate the workplace.

Why Networking Is Important

In spite of all the business literature that asserts the value of networking, many blacks avoid it because they don't believe it is important to them. As people move up in their careers, however, they often come to realize they were mistaken. "I just didn't get into it," says Joanna Gayle, a vice president in a major bank. "I didn't fancy it or realize the importance. If I work late, I just want to go home. [Networking is] not my culture, but now I realize it's important." Paul Camp, a manufacturing manager, had a similar realization: "I see now that I hurt myself in my career advancement, at least early on. I did not participate in management clubs. I paid my membership dues, but I never attended any of the functions."

Ironically, it is because of the many difficulties African Americans face in the workplace that networking is of paramount importance; it can be a major aid to maneuvering around these obstacles. Networking is vital because participants can gather and share information, learn about options and opportunities, learn about pitfalls, increase their visibility, gain opportunities to display credibility and ability, gain support, and forge alliances.

Gathering and Sharing Information

Gathering and sharing information is a key function of networking and is becoming increasingly critical to the navigation of corporate relationships. However, because African Americans often lack access to key networks and because they often distrust or are distrusted by some of their colleagues, African American employees can find information difficult to obtain. Learning to expand and use the networks at your disposal is a critical way to increase your corporate knowledge. Information is like money: the more you have, the more you can get.

Learning About Options and Opportunities

Through networking, people often learn of jobs or projects with which they would like to be involved. Through networking, people discover information helpful to their careers. African Americans often say they don't know what is going on in corporate areas beyond their normal areas of responsibility. HR consultant Jamaal Laker, for example, says he did not socialize at work nor did he pay attention to his colleagues' comings and goings. "I didn't care what they were doing," says Laker, "so I'm always the last one to know gossip. And because of that lack of interaction with others, I didn't find out people were going for training, and maybe the thing was that the only people [the boss] was sending to training were those that asked."

Learning About Pitfalls

For those who network effectively, learning what did not go well for others may be as important as learning best practices. African Americans find that through networking, particularly with other blacks, they can learn about both the general pitfalls in the organization and the racially sensitive ones. In one of our early African-American Leadership Program seminars, a grizzled veteran of the race-work wars spoke up on this topic. After admitting that he had come across as an embittered man for much of the class, he urged his fellow participants to listen to the instructors and to each other. "Listen," he said, his eyes glistening, "and don't step on the mines that I've stepped on. Don't end up a bitter old man like me."

Increasing Visibility

If you wish to move ahead in business, it is important to enhance your visibility. Before people can develop an interest in promoting a manager, white or black, they need to know that this manager exists. Networking is a way of gaining or enhancing visibility. Networking gives blacks a chance to be seen by a greater number of people than those in their personal circles and spreads the word about their skills and accomplishments. African Americans often feel they are invisible; this aspect of networking can help blacks be more visible. Such networking, of course, may present challenges for the many black managers who view this as "playing politics." However, one might counter that those who aren't known aren't grown. If you aren't recognized by name or on sight, your probability of success is significantly reduced because yours will not be the name that comes to mind for future opportunities or advancement.

Gaining Opportunities to Display Credibility and Ability

Enhanced visibility also gives an individual the chance to show himself or herself to be a credible team member—one who can be counted on to do the job right. Again, for African Americans the issue of credibility is particularly tough because many blacks feel that their credibility is fleeting and that they must repeatedly prove themselves. "You're always being second-guessed," says Maurice Greene, "every day is a start over." Gaining large-scale visibility, or at least visibility in the eyes of those more influential than them, can help African Americans promote and retain their credibility by placing their actions in a public forum and thereby making those actions a part of the institution's history.

Gaining Support

By getting to know more people and displaying one's skill level, individuals who network gain support in the workplace. African Americans often feel unsupported; networking can increase the number of people who know and support them. This support can come not only from other blacks. It is a function of familiarity, and to increase it, people have to let others get to know them.

Sometimes support is less about moving up and more about finding a safe haven in a foreign environment. Helen Thompson, program manager at a major chemical company, remembers going to an organizational meeting where, as usual, the whites vastly outnumbered the blacks. "At this particular meeting we [African Americans] decided that we were going to be together, which is something we never do because we always tried to make sure that everybody is comfortable, so we mix and mingle, but we never interact with each other." So, even though the group of blacks attracted a lot of attention, these individuals felt a little less alone than they had at previous meetings.

Forging Alliances

Networking is integrally entwined with other work behaviors, as is explained in more depth in the chapters on mentoring and political savvy. Networking is a strong component of forging political alliances. Alliances differ from friendships in that they are strategic relationships that form around specific issues. By discovering common cause with other groups, African Americans can strengthen their individual and group positions, particularly when they are trying to get the organization to change a system or create a new one. All groups involved in an alliance become stronger as a result of their joining, enjoying greater leverage and visibility and having a louder voice.

What Is Unique to the Black Experience

There are forces that deter and discourage blacks from networking together. Among these forces are the inherent tensions between individual lifestyle needs and the need to practice corporate biculturalism—that is, the dynamics created when one must straddle different personal and professional worlds. Other pressures spring from the perceptions and the standards of a traditionally white corporate workplace that does not understand or welcome difference and that is sometimes threatened by it.

The Personal Cost of Networking

The question for African Americans is not always, *Can* I network? but, What is the cost of doing so? For many blacks, pursuing opportunities to expand professional corporate networks may involve giving up culturally rewarding or socially and emotionally enhancing opportunities. For instance, Robert Stanley says he very consciously chose to continue living in an urban area even though his regional office is located in the suburbs and his main office in another state. "We chose to live in the city because our family, friends, church, everything we do is in the city. If I wanted to just further my career, I would live thirty miles north. It's a whole other take on work-life balance. . . . Whites don't have to give up personal stuff." Stanley adds that he knows there are consequences for his actions and that he has tried to compensate for them with other behaviors. For example, he believes that if he lived in the suburbs, he would probably be invited to the informal affairs held by his colleagues. To make up for missing those opportunities, he tries to have lunch with a different person at least once a month and breakfast twice a month. He has also begun playing golf for the same reasons.

"The Show's Over" at 5 P.M.

Many African Americans don't want to network because they don't want to maintain their bicultural façade any longer than they absolutely must. In almost every African-American Leadership Program in which networking has been discussed, someone has said, "I work with [whites] all day; I don't see any need to spend my evenings with them too." For many African Americans, it's more about having to wear the mask or be on guard for extra periods of time than any dislike of their white colleagues. Helen Thompson echoes this sentiment. She says that when it comes to networking, "my day ends at five o'clock, and you know, I've been with these people all day and when I get done I'm just going home." Both comments reveal that for many African Americans being around whites is not relaxing—it is work. Whether this is true because of perceived or real cultural differences between the groups, because of discomfort with the settings in which networking takes place, or because of distrust between the groups, for many blacks networking with whites can be a chore because they do not feel they can let down their guard and be themselves.

The Lunchtime Experience

Although networking with other blacks is a source of support, blacks are often discouraged from networking with each other too much. Both black and white colleagues have told new black employees point-blank that they should not be seen fraternizing with other blacks too often. Such behaviors, the old employees say, may be viewed by higher-ups with disapproval. Blacks may also receive this message more subtly. Indeed, blacks seen talking together often draw the attention of white colleagues. This attention may come in many forms, such as a chuckle and the question, "What are you all talking about?" or the comment, "You sure do have a lot to say to each other." One African American, a vice president in his organization, said that when he is with two other black people in the office, he mockingly pretends to bounce a basketball. For many whites, he jests, "Bouncing a ball is the only legitimate reason more than two blacks can have for getting together."

When a number of whites congregate, rarely do they receive strange looks or comments simply because they are white and together. Yet for blacks this is a routine experience, one that suggests to them, again, that they may really not belong—and if they do, their presence may be judged with greater scrutiny.

What You as African Americans Can Do

If you have aspirations for leadership, one of the first and best things you can do is to establish and grow a network. Realize that, yes, net-

---

What African Americans Can Do About Networking

Recognize the importance of networking early in your career.

Take responsibility for not networking.

Network with other blacks.

Network outside the black community too.

Forge meaningful alliances.

Don't believe every slight is intentional.

Stretch your comfort zone.

Be willing to trust.

Find commonalities and safe personal issues to share.

Speak to others so they can hear you.

Remember the people with whom you network.

---

working is indeed working, but it can have personal as well as professional rewards. Through networks, you might discover trusted agents (Chapter Four) and mentors (Chapter Six), strategic people who can support you on the path to success. Networking can also help you become more engaged and establish conduits that will allow you to do a better job.

Recognize the importance of networking early in your career. Repeatedly in our interviews, black leaders said that to their dismay they did not see the value of networking early in their careers. They realized its importance only after recognizing that networking was helping others move ahead of them. What many young, black professionals don't realize is that networking is not about "kissing up" to whites or to the power structure. It is about cultivating relationships that can be emotionally supportive, supply you with valuable information, and grant access and visibility that make you more effective. The more visibility you have, the greater the number of opportunities that may be available to you.

Take responsibility for not networking.   If you choose not to network, be sure you do so with an understanding of the consequences. Although we would all like to believe that people get opportunities because they work hard and deserve it, we all know that people are more likely to get opportunities if someone knows them or can vouch for them. To avoid networking is to limit the number of people who know you. Helen Thompson says that blacks at her company found "that a lot of networking went on at these cocktail parties and golf outings and all these other things, and when you say you're going to make a conscious decision to remove yourself from those activities, you cut off information that you need, and so if you want to do that, fine, but recognize the downside—the consequences."

Network with other blacks.   In spite of beliefs that networking with other blacks can be detrimental to your career, research findings and common sense suggest otherwise. As stated earlier in this chapter, a CCL study on networking patterns revealed that blacks who network significantly with other blacks are perceived as more effective leaders than their black colleagues who network less with other blacks. When it comes to gathering information about the challenges and impact of being black in your organization, whom better to ask than an African American who has already trod the path upon which you are embarking? These are the people you need to tap for this type of information. Look to network both inside and outside your company and your industry, because you never know where you might find insight, support, and information.

Network outside the black community too.   Although networking with other blacks is a good strategy, networking outside the black community is also important. Of course we are talking about both the personal and professional community. Unless your organization is entirely black, there are other people, viewpoints, and experiences in your organization that you should try to access. To restrict yourself to any one group is to limit the information you may receive and thus your opportunities. It can create major blind spots in your awareness that can become problems for you. Tyrone Billington, for example, has joined civic organizations such as his local Rotary club to give himself access to different points of views and opportunities. "I serve on several boards," he says; "I put myself in these situations. I'm there. This way I'm establishing access. This is not to say it's easy. There are times I feel isolated when I'm in those situations. No one said it would be easy." Connections such as these serve a critical function, providing you with opportunities to build relationships, gather and share information, and negotiate with others who are different from you—often in an environment where the consequences may not be as risky as those in the workplace. At the end of the day any opportunities to develop new skills and to become more comfortable in networking with others can prove invaluable.

Forge meaningful alliances. Find ways to ally yourself with others in your corporation. For example, if other minority groups have networking organizations, work together with them on similar interests. Support them on their issues even when those issues do not directly affect you. In discussing his company's African American and women's affinity groups, chemical company manager Johnson McDaniel suggested that if members of such groups "worked together to bring these networks together and spoke as a single voice or a single network, it would change dramatically how things are done in corporate America." By allying themselves with others, blacks give themselves the opportunity to see issues in more complex ways and to look beyond the ways only they are affected. We believe this will help blacks engage in and more fully understand strategic ways of thinking and solving problems.

Don't believe every slight is intentional. One of the barriers to networking is that some African Americans are thin-skinned when it comes to certain comments made by their coworkers, particularly their white coworkers. They often feel that any misstep by others is a *purposeful* racial slight. There are certainly times when racial slights are intentional. However, more times than not, people say things or make mistakes that come across as racial when these individuals are actually unaware of the impact of their comments. Although ignorance is not an excuse for hurtful behavior, tolerance may help you to determine when there is no malicious intent behind a slight. Sometimes a mistake is just a mistake. Not every molehill is worthy of being built into a mountain. There are plenty of mountains out there without your helping to build more.

Stretch your comfort zone. Networking effectively can mean stretching your comfort zone—trying different things and pursuing alternatives that may not be natural avenues for you. For those of you who don't drink alcohol, this might mean going to the local bar just because the other members of your team do (and drinking sparkling water or juice). In a similar way, you can stretch your comfort zone around associating with whites. The fact that you have rarely done so doesn't mean you can't change your behavior now. You may be surprised at what you have in common with whites and how much fun you can have together. By stretching your comfort zone and trying new things, you can reap benefits that might otherwise have gone unnoticed or remained out of your reach. Keep in mind that any new behaviors may feel awkward or even unpleasant at first. If on your first try a situation turns out to be downright awful, try it again anyway just to be sure. Many things are difficult the first time around because we don't know what to expect or we do or say the wrong things. The next time out, or the time after that, you may discover yourself becoming more comfortable in the situation. You never know, you may even enjoy it—at the very least, you will survive.

Be willing to trust. Find ways to help people trust you and find ways to trust them back. Because networking is about building relationships, it revolves around trust. One way to encourage people to trust you is to get them talking about themselves, then respond positively to them—let them see that you are a human with a number of the same needs and concerns that they have. They have families, hopes, and dreams as do you. As you find ways to engender their trust, you need to find ways to trust them too. The same techniques that you use with them can be good for you. Listen to what they are saying. See them as people with foibles and strengths similar to yours. Consulting firm director Marcella Watkins advises that "the first thing" is to get beyond first impressions and stereotypes and to bring each other into "a different realm—the realm of being human. I'm not what they see at first, a black woman with short hair. It is in the dialogue of talking that we can begin to suspend notions about each other. We can start on a different page."

Find commonalities and safe personal issues to share. Often black people fear that if they network they have to share all of their personal business. This is not true. You can share only to the degree that you feel comfortable, and usually others will still feel that you have opened up a great deal. One way to open the door to sharing is to find commonalities. If you have children and the other person has children, talk about children. Usually, such conversations are not highly personal, but they set a foundation for you to get to know each other. Danielle Rogers, a human resource director, says, "I will pick a particular person I have something in common with and then I will share what's safe—like my twin grandbabies. . . . Now when people talk about the twins, it's as if they know me."

Speak to others so they can hear you. Part of networking with people is giving them the best opportunity to understand what you are saying. Maurice Greene says that part of networking is getting people to buy into your leadership. One of the ways that people can do this is to talk to others in "the way they live." If someone is very direct, approach him or her directly. If another person is amiable, attempt to create an open, friendly relationship with him or her. By talking to people where they live, you give both them and yourself the best opportunity to be heard.

Remember the people with whom you network. Not the least important part of networking is remembering the people you have met and following up with them. Keith Shields writes on the back of a business card or notes in his organizer some pertinent data about each person he meets, such as their sales goals, hobbies, spouse's and children's names, whether they talk quickly or make jokes, and where he met them. He also makes sure to follow up with people by e-mail within a few weeks after meeting them. Today there are a number of programs for personal computers that can expedite this task. Remember, one of the keys to networking is to give the impression that you remember more than just someone's name and to be memorable to others yourself. Other people we interviewed suggested using a new acquaintance's name frequently during the first meeting, as a way to commit the name to memory. Yet others suggested finding a common interest that can serve as a platform on which to build a relationship—sports, children, or having the same hometown.

What You as Colleagues Can Do

Helping others expand their networks is also a way to expand your own. As you have probably experienced, networking is an exponential endeavor: developing one relationship leads to many more. By having African Americans and others who are different from you in your network, you increase the variety of information sources you have and thus your exposure to information and opportunity.

Don't be disconcerted by a group of African Americans. It is pretty safe to say that when blacks get together, they are not discussing how to overthrow the workplace or the nation. Generally, they are talking about home, work, play, sports, and family—the same things you probably discuss with your friends and colleagues. Admittedly, sometimes they may be talking about how white folks don't "get it." But the point is that as a non-black person, you don't have to be concerned about their conversations. You also don't have

---

What Colleagues Can Do About Networking

Don't be disconcerted by a group of African Americans.

Create opportunities for others to come into the inner circle.

Understand that being fair and being equal are not always the same.

Meet blacks on their terms as well as yours.

Recognize that networking advice for blacks often works for others as well.

---

to insert yourself into their conversations, and you don't have to make comments or jokes about their being together. Treat these occasions just as you would want someone to treat conversations between you and your like colleagues. They are a non-issue.

Create opportunities for others to come into the inner circle. If you are part of the inner circle of your work group, department, branch, or organization, look at your network and consider how diverse it is. Whose perspectives are not being represented? Find ways to bring others into the group. Invite them to sit in on meetings; to make presentations; to join you for coffee, for breakfast, or for a drink after work; or to do any number of things that are appropriate to their roles, possibilities, or the situation. Recognize as you do this that you are doing a favor not only for them but also for yourself and your network. By bringing in others, you bring in new sources of information and new ways to analyze a situation. Remember, this strategy is most likely to be successful when you bring others into the network because you know they can add something, rather than bringing them in because you feel it is a "good deed."

Understand that being fair and being equal are not always the same. A clear example of how the fact that fair and equal are not the same thing plays out in networking in Robert Stanley's story, related earlier in this chapter, about how his boss and a colleague network at their country club. Yes, the way is open for Stanley to become a member of the country club, so it is arguably fair that his boss and colleague meet there. However, this club's history and practice make it very unlikely that Stanley would ever want to join. In this regard, Stanley's access to his boss is not equal to that of his white colleague. As you become aware of equal yet unfair practices in your network, do something about them. If after-hours socializing takes place at culturally loaded places like country clubs or bars, suggest a change in locale. If your lunch invitations go out only to those who work nearest you, extend them to others as well, even those outside your department.

Meet blacks on their terms as well as yours. Most networking is done on terms set by whites rather than by blacks or other groups. This practice occurs largely because whites usually outnumber other groups in positions of leadership, and so networking occurs on the terms that seem natural to the majority. The problem is that these terms are often not natural for the non-whites in the group. If you are invited to network in places and ways that are comfortable to non-whites, you will benefit from accepting the invitation. Tyrone Billington tells about inviting a group of coworkers to his bar after joining them after-hours at their bar on many occasions. "They said no," Billington says. "They were fearful. They wouldn't buy it. They would have been the minority and they couldn't deal with it." Though the incident happened many years ago, Billington still remembers it with a great deal of bitterness. He felt his colleagues assumed he would take them to a place where they wouldn't be safe, which he would never have done. He also believed they weren't willing to see his world even though they expected him to see theirs. The bottom line is that if networking is going to be effective, it must go both ways.

Recognize that networking advice for blacks often works for others as well. Networking suggestions we have made for African

Americans, such as stretching your comfort zone, forging alliances, helping people trust you and trusting others, and not limiting your network to people who share your race, are excellent advice for everyone. To get the full benefit of networking, you should be willing to stretch outside of yourself and to fully engage others.

Networking is a critical broad-based skill that paves the way for deeper professional relationships. One of the most powerful relationships African Americans can cultivate in the workplace is the relationship with a mentor. As we discuss in the next chapter, learning to refine your networking skill and using that skill to develop a relationship with a mentor or to become a mentor is equally important as networking itself—both for your development as a leader and for the development of African Americans in the corporate sector.

6

Growing and Grooming Leaders

Marianne Farley, a new sales manager, believes she needs a mentor. There are *things* she just seems to be missing. She doesn't quite know what these things are, but she knows she doesn't have them or isn't doing them. All around her, colleagues seem to be passing her up, moving ahead. It's as if they have a road map for success, one to which she hasn't been made privy. And even though she thinks a mentor might be able to help her find her personal map, she's not quite sure that she can get a mentor or that she even knows how to go about getting one. Marianne is thirty-five and black and everyone above her in the hierarchy is white. As she looks around she notices that mentors appear to choose their protégés. Thus far, none of them has chosen anyone black.

Bob Jefferson, operations director, is feeling pretty good. He's just come out of a very productive session with Will Hemlock, his vice president. Bob had gone in to talk to Will about financial reports, and their conversation had extended to lunch and dinner meetings. Will gave Bob all kinds of tips on how to work the conversation and how to read the group he would be facing and was charged with influencing. Bob smiled as he thought to himself, "I'm black, black as night, and Will is white as snow, and that's okay with me." At thirty-seven, Bob is moving up and he knows it. He had contemplated looking for a black mentor. In fact, he had the opportunity once, but passed it up. He wanted somebody white, somebody he believed had influence and power. Bob figured he couldn't get that from anyone black, so he continued to work hard and bide his time. When Will told Bob that if he had any questions, he could always come to him, Bob jumped at the chance. The way Bob saw it, for the times he needed support, he had black friends, but when what he wanted was information, he needed someone white, preferably a white male.

Ricky Ramsey, a logistics manager, wants a mentor, a black mentor. He figures he needs someone with whom he can relate. Ramsey considered trying to get a white mentor but dropped that idea pretty fast. "I couldn't trust him," Ricky thought, "he wouldn't know what it's like to be black. I need somebody to show me the ropes." Then Janet Smith, a senior director over Ricky's entire division and an African American, reached out to him. Janet has been with the company for ten years and she has been through the wars—she has been through much of the same "stuff" he is facing now. What impresses Ricky is that Janet has not only been through the wars, she has survived and thrived. He wants to thrive too, but first he has to learn how to survive. "This is going to work," he smiles. "Today is a good day."

These composite scenarios, using data from our surveys of African American leaders, speak to some of the issues and challenges that surround African American leaders and mentoring. The potentially most compelling question for many blacks, Should my mentor be black or white? often becomes moot as one realizes how few African American mentors are available in corporate America. The question suggests a broad choice that reality rarely proffers. As John Fernandez states in his book *Race, Gender and Rhetoric*, the reality is that mentors tend to choose to assist people who look like themselves; often this means someone who looks like them and with whom they can easily relate. Thus for African Americans the question switches from, Can I get a mentor who looks like me? to, Can I get a mentor at all? The former question is one white leaders do not usually have to ask; it is a fair assumption that their mentors can be white, like them, and, more times than not, male. Although this does not imply that no white leaders have minority mentors, the odds are that in the vast majority of mentoring situations, mentors will be white.

The question, Can I get a mentor? is a big one. If, as Fernandez suggests, people tend to mentor those who are like themselves, then minorities are apt to have fewer mentors to choose from or be chosen by. In spite of this, African Americans find the mentoring experience to be particularly salient in the development of their managerial careers, more so than their white colleagues do. In fact, the Center for Creative Leadership study Lessons of a Diverse Workforce reveals that African Americans find the mentoring experience to be particularly important. However the study doesn't ask the question, Is racial likeness necessary in a mentoring relationship?

Harvard professor David Thomas finds mentoring important in enhancing the careers of minority managers. In his article "The Truth About Mentoring Minorities: Race Matters," he provides several reasons why minority executives in particular benefit from mentoring relationships. Mentors provide critical support; among other things, they open doors to challenging assignments, give critical career advice and counsel, and appropriately confront those who unfairly criticize or stymie their protégés—particularly when such behaviors seem racially motivated. However, Thomas also reports that "a significant round of research shows that cross-race (as well as cross-gender) relationships can have difficulty forming, developing, and maturing." These challenges often stem from, among other things, negative stereotypes, the difficulty of identifying with mentors, and public scrutiny (because such relationships are rare).

Throughout this chapter, we explore challenges and opportunities as well as other factors that influence the mentoring relationships of African Americans in unique ways.

What Mentoring Looks Like

Mentoring can be simply described as a purposeful developmental relationship, generally between two individuals. It may occur in a relationship set up explicitly by the organization within a formal mentoring program, or it may develop informally between two people over time. Mentoring relationships usually include an expressed or implied expectation of commitment on the part of both mentor and protégé to the protégé's development.

Although this describes many corporate mentoring relationships, for African Americans, mentoring often takes on a familial flavor. At the beginning of The African-American Leadership Program, we ask participants to acknowledge those who have mentored them. Overwhelmingly, participants most frequently credit family members for contributing to their success and *professional* development. Perhaps because the number of blacks in the executive ranks is low or because many African American executives are still first- or second-generation corporate managers, family members often serve as important mentors for many of them. The significance of family as a developmental base is also mentioned by participants in our mentoring research. Monica Stewart, a medical research team leader, cites her mother, saying, "She was a mentor because she was an administrator, planner, organizer, and manager, and she showed me how to do those kinds of things just from growing up and watching her in those kinds of environments." Likewise, Tina Williams, a clinical psychologist, says her mother taught her to go after whatever she wanted. Her mother also said, "we have to work for whatever we get," and encouraged Tina to have high expectations.

Though this may seem the same sage counsel many parents give their children, we believe there is a twist. In our discussions with black professionals, embedded in the advice their parents doled out, along with the strategic tactics and poignant encouragement, was hope. The advice many African American parents have given their children for surviving in an often-hostile world has been mingled with the belief that "there will be better days," the hope that those days will come in their children's lifetime, and the sadness that the odds have been against it. Telling black children born in the forties, fifties, and even sixties that they could be what they wanted to be and that they should never quit was as much wishful thinking as it was sound advice.

Again, because they cannot find mentors at work, many blacks have broadened the scope of their mentoring net. Often African Americans seek out opportunities to mentor and to be mentored through their community, church, or other social settings. Johnson McDaniel, the chemical company manager, for example, finds the church to be a forum "where you can spread ideas and where you can do a lot of mentoring."

Formal Mentoring

Recognizing the benefits of mentoring, some organizations have instituted formal programs that pair leaders and protégés. Although well intentioned, these programs often fall short because of limited commitment or feelings of intrusion or duty-bound obligation in one or both parties. In addition, African Americans may feel their safety and openness are compromised if they are teamed with someone with whom they have no more in common than having their names matched through the formal mentoring program. Even when serving as mentors, blacks find formal programs daunting. "I have been assigned mentees," says Marcella Watkins, a consulting firm director. "That doesn't work." Gayle Harris, a corporate training analyst, agrees with Watkins, explaining, "You can't force somebody to be a mentor. [Companies] have these mentoring programs, and they put people together, and people don't want to do it." In addition to these challenges, some African Americans may be looking specifically for mentors who can give them social support and who can help them identify the problems that may befall a black manager, goals often unmet through formal mentoring programs.

Although flawed in many aspects, formal mentoring programs do attempt to address the inadequacies of the informal mentoring process. Formal programs have matched people who then developed strong working or personal relationships. Also, these programs have given protégés enhanced organizational visibility and exposure to ideas that they might not have ordinarily received. Interestingly, Fernandez reports that although about 40 percent of U.S. corporations have formal mentoring programs, only about 20 percent of employees believe that their companies have such programs.

Informal Mentoring

Informal mentoring results from purposeful personal relationships. These relationships develop because someone recognizes something in another person that he or she wishes to nurture or to learn from. Informal mentoring works at least in part because of the *chemistry* that exists between the participants. However, it is because informal networking is discretionary that many African Americans and others who do not fit the traditional mold feel they have fewer opportunities to become involved in these mentoring relationships. Deborah Carter, an executive for an international oil company, feels that because she is black and a woman she has had few role models and few people who were willing to reach out to help her in her development. "I had to prove myself first before they would take a risk and say, 'I am going to help this person. I am going to sponsor this person.'" Carter believes that her white colleagues did not have to prove themselves before they got mentors. Instead, the mentors "were willing to take a risk on them, to go ahead and give them the opportunity and say, 'We'll see if they fail or succeed.'"

Similarly, Marcella Watkins says she has never had a real mentoring relationship. Instead, she has learned to find mentoring nuggets—lessons that have come to her in bites or from unexpected sources. One nugget, for example, came from an older, white man who just came up to her one day and said, "Always seek to know what you want because somebody might ask you and give you the opportunity to get it." He never said anything else to her. "He said this right before he retired," she said. "We had a connection. He was not publicly comfortable with mentoring this black woman, but he appreciated me and he wanted to show his appreciation."

Although there are stories of informal mentoring relationships with whites that have gone askew, there are also those that have worked out well. Keith Shields, senior vice president of a financial institution, remembers how he went through a rotational program when he first began to work at a bank. During one portion of the rotation, Shields drilled one of the managers with question after question. "Who did you rely on in the bank?" Shields asked the man, and then followed it up with, "Who do I?" After their session, the manager told Shields to come to him if he had further questions, after which Shields thought to himself, "I'm not going to let that go." The manager became someone Shields could rely on. Later, when Shields and his own boss were in conflict, Shields's mentor asked Shields to join his department.

Why Mentoring Is Important

The stories of Carter, Watkins, Shields, and others explain in real terms why mentoring is important. Through mentoring, you can receive visibility, strategies for success, support, access, and exposure. Mentoring helps you borrow the wisdom of others. By sharing their knowledge, mentors impart valuable lessons of experience and guidance to ensure that those being mentored do not have to travel the same path the mentors did. In Keith Shields's case, mentoring also provided a port in a storm. Once Deborah Carter finally got a mentor, she found that her languishing career began to flourish. Under the mentor's guidance, Carter learned how to look at her business in a different light. "He taught me to think globally instead of just looking at what was before me," she said. "The other thing he taught me, or tried to teach me—I'm still working on it, was to enjoy my job and not take it so seriously."

It is because mentoring can help smooth so many paths and subtly change so many careers that the fact that so few blacks and others outside the traditional managerial norm have access to it becomes critical. Although many African Americans we interviewed say they have been mentored, many others say they have not. Sam

Masters puts it this way, "Unfortunately, I think much of what I've learned has been kind of self-developing." Masters and others like him are forced to pick up what information they can. Though they may still succeed, they have to do it the hard way, stepping on land mines that others know exist and discovering all over again ways of doing business that others have uncovered previously.

What Is Unique to the Black Experience

As we have stated throughout this chapter, mentoring can be a powerful experience—especially for African Americans and other nontraditional leaders. However, organizations may use blacks as mentors for other blacks to further organizational goals. Even though this is similar to the organization's use of any of its employees, being asked to mentor just because you are black can be very stressful. Blacks may find such assignments limiting or because they are so highly scrutinized may feel particularly vulnerable if they make mistakes. Or they may struggle with multiple loyalties—for example, to other African Americans, to their organizations, and to their own success. This often places them under enormous pressure as they struggle with the question of which loyalty comes first in any given situation. It is not uncommon for black leaders to struggle with, on the one hand, telling younger African American employees hard truths about the company and, on the other hand, being loyal to the company and hiding these truths so the employees will not look elsewhere for work. In addition, because the mentoring bond can be so strong and so personal, the impact of race on the relationship can be unique. Often when people think of race, their minds jump to cross-racial issues. It is important to recognize, however, that race also has an impact in same-race pairings—sometimes for the better, sometimes not.

Blacks Are Expected to Mentor Other Blacks

For some blacks, mentoring other African Americans may not be as much a personal choice as an organizational expectation. Oftentimes, the company assumes that on top of their regular job responsibilities, leaders will also take care of the needs of those in their ethnic community. Mel Kaitt, a special projects director at a major chemical company, says he was given the responsibility to "'shepherdly' manage . . . without job credits and without recognition." Although Kaitt wanted to work with his constituency in the organization, he still resented the idea that he *had* to do this because he was black. "When you feel like it's expected of you," he says, "because of your position of leadership, or expected of you because of your stature with a network of people, then [you start asking] 'when did it become a burden versus a task of joy?'"

There Are Too Few Blacks to Act as Mentors

The issue of having "like" mentors available to validate one's experiences, provide guidance, or ensure that one is getting fair exposure or opportunities plagues black managers. In our survey and interviews, the scarcity of potential black mentors was noticeable. When asked whether their organizations had high-ranking African Americans, and whether those people were willing to mentor other blacks, many respondents simply answered no to the first question. "There aren't any," said one participant, "one manager and no executive." "There are no African American executives," said another. Added a third, "There are very few [African Americans] at the vice president level. Some at the director level, but less than 1 percent." Says pharmacy manager Nelson Evans of the number of blacks with authority in his organization, "you can count them on one hand, minus the thumb." If blacks have to count on other blacks to mentor them, then the numbers show that many African American managers will have to go without mentoring.

Some Blacks Don't Want to Mentor Other Blacks

Although African Americans often malign those blacks who decline to mentor black colleagues, we uncovered a variety of reasons why people may make this choice. When we asked, as we just described, whether individuals' organizations had high-ranking African Americans, and whether those people were willing to mentor other blacks, most people who answered yes to the first part of the question also said that these black leaders in their organization were willing to mentor. Those respondents who said they had black leaders who were unwilling to mentor other blacks gave a variety of reasons for those decisions:

- These leaders made it on their own and believe other blacks should do the same.
- These leaders are too busy.
- These leaders are too geographically separated from other blacks to act as mentors.
- These leaders fear reprisal from management.
- These leaders don't want to appear to be favoring other blacks.

Often blacks think that when black leaders do not mentor African Americans it is for racial reasons—they are trying to distance themselves, they fear reprisal from white managers, and so forth. Although these reasons may be true in some instances, our data suggest that the reasons may be broader. The fact that blacks may be geographically separated from other blacks or are simply too busy to mentor anyone are other valid, albeit obvious, reasons. That race is so ever-present in the lives and thinking of black professionals is disconcerting. Clearly it is as hard for many African Americans to see the world without race as it is for the world to see African Americans without it.

The Glass Ceiling Can Be Broken

For some African Americans, black mentors are role models, a tangible sign that it is possible to break through the "glass ceiling." One survey respondent said it was important to have an African

American mentor because it served as an affirmation, letting "you know that the upper-level management will promote effective African American people." Having high-ranking African Americans as mentors gives the black protégés tangible and readily available evidence that blacks can make it into the senior ranks of corporate America. This evidence, coupled with books and business articles spotlighting African American CEOs and senior executives, gives life to their hopes and makes their aspirations more than pipe dreams. For some these examples of success suggest that race may not be as high a hurdle as they have previously believed. This new mind-set further challenges individuals to check for other opportunities for growth, development, and success.

Should Your Mentor Be Racially Like You?

Figure 6.1 highlights the various mentoring relationship preferences of African Americans. Although some blacks tend to think other African Americans can provide the best support for them in the corporate environment, the vast majority of those we surveyed stated that it does not matter or that they would like to have both a white and black mentor. As one respondent quipped, "I'd like one of each, please," as if hoping that a selection of mentors was available and willing to support his various needs. Unfortunately that is not usually the case.

The vast majority of the people in our survey and interviews felt that a mentor did not have to be the same race they were. Often people said that what mattered most in a mentor was the ability to "help, advise, and relate to" what the protégé needed to know and understand. Many also said that the chemistry of the relationship needed to be right or that the mentor needed to have enough influence and know-how to effectively assist the protégé's learning. Many of those we interviewed said non-blacks, typically white men, had mentored them, resulting in very good experiences.

Wilson Davis, lead technical specialist for a major tobacco firm, describes his relationship with one of his mentors, who eventually

FIGURE 6.1. Mentors and African Americans.

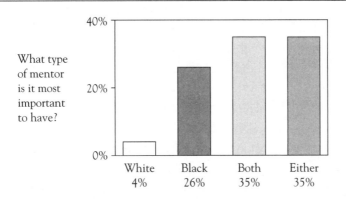

What type of mentor is it most important to have?

| White | Black | Both | Either |
| 4% | 26% | 35% | 35% |

became his best friend, as one of these positive interactions. Davis and his mentor, a white man, hit it off immediately because they both liked the same kind of jazz. They would go to the mentor's house and play their saxophones together. Later, they would go to black jazz clubs where they could play. "[Because I was] hanging with him," Davis says, "people began to assume that I knew more than I did, and he did his best to make sure they understood that I knew a lot more than they gave me credit for." Similarly, Larry Wiggins, a human resource manager, counts an Asian American woman as one of his staunchest supporters. "She is and was and has always been a very strong supporter and mentor," he says. "And I think because of the similarities that we share, there was a genuine concern that she had for my development, and also we were able to communicate."

Though most of our survey respondents did not state a preference for the race of their mentor, those who did overwhelmingly preferred a black mentor. An African American mentor, many said, would understand their experience more fully and would be able to guide them more effectively than would a white mentor. Darlene Winchester, diversity manager of a financial institution, reports of her rich experience with black mentors: "They can better understand where I'm coming from—nine times out of ten they have been there too. I could relate to an African American better and hopefully they to me. I learned the most about being a professional and how to deal with the challenges of being an African American professional from other African Americans." She adds that these were people who had gone before her, "stepped on land mines and gotten blown up and put back together."

Although their numbers were relatively few, some survey respondents said that if given a choice, they would choose a white mentor over others, specifically over a black mentor. This choice was almost always made for utilitarian reasons. These respondents perceived white mentors as having more authority, influence, credibility, and access; consequently they saw white mentors as their key to these same attributes. "I would prefer a Caucasian," said one respondent, "who will offer me insight into the other side or hidden agenda." Another respondent wanted a white mentor because he or she would have a "better introduction to higher-ups. A better understanding of where I need to get to." A third respondent wrote, "A Caucasian is definitely more of value to the organization. It validates you."

Most respondents said they would prefer to have both a black and white mentor or one of each. For these people, the reasons for having mentors from both races incorporated the reasons why others chose one race over the other. In essence most people who said they wanted at least one of each wanted black mentors for psychosocial support or to learn the racial, political lay of the land and white mentors to help them move up in the organization. One interviewee explained, "A Caucasian is more in tune with overall politics and can help you fit in. You need an African American to give you real scoop from an African American perspective." Another respondent said you should have an "African American for grounding and dynamics impacted by or impacting racial perceptions and issues. You need a Caucasian to get a sponsor who can move easily [and] exercise hiring/development and promotional opportunities."

Surprisingly to us, these data illustrated how clearly blacks saw other African Americans as being useful almost solely in the area of emotional support and race relations and understanding. Again and again we saw black respondents saying they would go to blacks for help in finding the land mines but to whites for help in climbing the ladder of success. The fallacy in this viewpoint is that although the number of African Americans in executive positions is not high, they *do* exist. Despite this, many African Americans seem to discount the influence and power these black leaders have garnered.

What You as African Americans Can Do

Whether you are looking for a mentor or already have one, challenge yourself to broaden your thinking regarding mentors and stretch yourself to cultivate them in different, opportune places. Step outside quick judgments based on race, job description, or management position. Evaluate what others have to offer by clearly considering your needs and others' strengths and wisdom. And of course, be willing to give back. You might find support or information in the most unlikely of places.

Be clear about your needs. When you are looking for a mentor, you want to have clarity about your personal and professional needs. Once you understand these needs, you can choose a mentor more effectively. Your needs may range from wanting emotional support to learning new information to understanding how to better use the information you receive. One area black managers should consider prior to entering into mentoring relationships is the importance to them of being able to address issues of race. After studying mentoring partnerships, David Thomas of Harvard University finds that black-white mentoring pairs can develop close mentoring relationships if both parties prefer the same strategy for handling race. If both parties wish to avoid racial conversations, the mentoring pair can develop an extremely close color-blind relationship. Similarly, if both partners wish to discuss race directly and the implications it may have for their careers and relationship, they too can develop a very compelling personal relationship. What is problematic is the situation in which one partner wishes to avoid racial discussions and the other wishes to deal with race head on. In these instances the mentoring relationship may yield professional information, but it is not likely to yield personal closeness. Thomas also found that the decision to avoid or to discuss race was usually determined by the preference of the mentor, not the protégé.

Don't limit mentoring partners. When selecting white mentors, recognize that the relationship can be more than purely utilitarian. You *can* get support from white mentors—and even though it may not take the same form as the support you would receive from black colleagues, that does not mean it will not be as good. When you consider black mentors, be careful not to limit the relationship to emotional support and racial surveillance. Many African Americans do have influence in their workplaces and wield it with skill. Be willing to recognize their expertise and learn from them. Darlene Winchester had such an experience and says it was well worth her while. She described her mentor, a black woman, as being "nurturing, tough, honest, and demanding and encouraging . . . everything that a good manager should be."

Although African Americans may not have a lot of high-ranking black mentors from which to choose, they are likely to have a substantial reservoir of non-executive mentors. It is a mistake to think that only people who have official titles understand the system or have information that's worth sharing. Many people tell stories of the custodian or cook or security guard who taught them lessons about perseverance or the perennial middle manager who explained exactly how the system worked in their particular company. To ignore these people and their information is to limit potentially rich sources of knowledge. African Americans also need to remember that mentors do not have to be black or white. As the workplace becomes increasingly diverse, we all have to be open to mentoring and being mentored by people of many nationalities and

---

What African Americans Can Do About Mentoring

Be clear about your needs.

Don't limit mentoring partners.

Don't choose mentors just because they are black.

Be willing to be a mentor, not just a protégé.

Don't be ruled by others' expectations.

Don't label other blacks.

Challenge your organization.

---

ethnic backgrounds. Just as blacks can bring a different perspective to the mentoring relationship, so can others. Because African Americans are so used to the black-white dynamic, they may dismiss other players and be blind to the fact that these others have information, influence, and access. You overlook these colleagues to your peril.

Don't choose mentors just because they are black. There can be many wonderful aspects to having a good mentoring relationship with an African American leader. Emotional support, racial advice, work tips, and career suggestions can all be part of the mentoring experience. However, don't expect this to happen just because your mentor or protégé is black. As Marcella Watkins says, "It can't happen just because we're black. There has to be something else." Keith Shields notes that a mentor doesn't have to be the same gender or race as you. Instead, you need to find some degree of connection with your potential mentor. "Color doesn't mean [the mentor] will understand you better," he says. "Someone of color may have a specific understanding of what you're going through—that shared experience alone doesn't translate into shared values in what a mentor brings."

Be willing to be a mentor, not just a protégé. A lot of African Americans are looking for a mentor for themselves without recognizing that they may be in a position to function as a mentor for someone else. Give yourself credit for the lessons you have learned and the experience you have gained by being willing to be open to opportunities to assist others. If you want to reach out to people, offer to take them to lunch, ask them to drop by your office, tell them to feel free to come by and talk to you if they have questions. Also be aware of your behavioral patterns. For example, are you willing to mentor only other African Americans? Are you open to mentoring those who are neither black nor white? Are you willing to mentor those who are white? If you want to work in a more equitable environment, you may have to lead the way in creating it.

Don't be ruled by others' expectations. One of the challenges of being black is that others have expectations for your behavior. Although we encourage you to give back to your community and to help African Americans and others to achieve success, we also believe that you cannot be ruled by others' expectations. If you are not careful, you will always be doing what family, friends, coworkers, the community, and the organization expect of you—you may not be doing what you want to do yourself. Down this road lies burnout and dissatisfaction. We are not suggesting that you turn completely away from others' desires and expectations, but we strongly urge that, first, you decide whether you believe what they believe. Second, you need to determine the appropriate balance between their expectations and your own. If you do not determine that balance and maintain it, the expectations of others will quickly become your burdens.

Don't label other blacks. A corollary to the idea that you don't have to live up to others' expectations is the notion that you should allow others to follow their own beliefs about how they should behave in the workplace. Oftentimes individuals do not know the pressures that affect how other individuals act. Throughout this chapter we have explored many reasons why black leaders may not mentor—many of those reasons deal less with a purposeful willingness not to mentor African Americans than with other considerations, such as available time, geography, and so forth. Consequently, if African American leaders choose not to be mentors, we argue that other blacks should not make assumptions about the reasons for these individuals' choices. Give these people the benefit of the doubt.

Challenge your organization. Although we suggest that there are limitations to many formal mentoring programs, we also acknowledge that they are a starting place. They give visibility opportunities to people who may not regularly get them. Formal mentoring programs may be particularly effective in places where the informal mentoring practices are very exclusive, thus limiting blacks or others who are different. We urge you to challenge organizational practices that do not provide, allow, or encourage mentoring relationships. If in your organization this means pushing for formal mentoring programs, please do so. If it means pushing to open the informal mentoring process, then work that path. Actively seek a mentor for yourself. Set yourself up as a mentor for others. Encourage your colleagues to do the same.

What You as Colleagues Can Do

The key to opening yourself up to effective cross-racial mentoring relationships is to look for similarities and at the same time recognize differences. Similarities might be found in someone's drive or spirit, professional interests or goals, life experiences, hobbies, or personal history. Differences might be any of those that have been outlined in this chapter or others unique to a person. By acknowledging and appreciating each individual's differences, you can open the door to a successful mentoring relationship.

See blacks as mentors and protégés. To ensure African Americans have ample opportunity to realize their true potential as both leaders and contributors, non-black colleagues need to see beyond race and be willing to view African Americans as potential mentors or protégés. For some this may be a stretch, as they may be unaware they are dismissing black colleagues and seeing connections only with individuals who are physically most like themselves. Step back and look at your organization: make an objective list of people who are acting as mentors and protégés. Do you notice any patterns? Examine your own motivations in accepting or soliciting mentors and protégés. Then take an honest look at the blacks in your organization and yourself. If you are a potential mentor, look for opportunities to add value to others' experience, fill noticeable skill or competency gaps, further develop professional potential, and encourage these valuable resources. If you are looking for another mentor, seek leaders who reflect qualities that you find effective or which you may lack, seek them whoever they are. Push your boundaries and talk with these potential mentors or protégés to explore partnering opportunities. Be willing to be uncomfortable. If you are in a formal mentoring program, fight any compulsion to rebel against serving as mentor to an African American or as the protégé of one. Take your mentorship seriously. Be open to suggestions, inputs, and insights. Be willing to see similarities in protégés and be willing to have two-way communications in which they can talk to you and you to them—this facilitates two-way learning. Don't get involved only out of duty; do it because you believe in it. Expect your mentor to grow and to challenge you, in racial awareness among other things. The mentoring process is about change, so allow your protégés to change and grow—and allow them to change you and help you grow.

Be willing to be uncomfortable. In order to have a black mentor or protégé, you need to be willing to be uncomfortable with the differences and challenges these relationships may bring. If you

---

What Colleagues Can Do About Mentoring

See blacks as mentors and protégés.

Be willing to be uncomfortable.

Communicate openly.

---

develop an open and trusting relationship with your counterpart, you may hear perceptions of the workplace that are foreign or even unbelievable to you. Don't turn away at the first sign of discomfort. In fact, seek out the source of it, and determine what you can learn about yourself and others. We suggest that as you get to know your mentor or protégé, you might even mention the discomfort you are feeling. However, you need to be sensitive in gauging whether this is a safe topic for your mentor or protégé to discuss. It may be that this person is also experiencing discomfort in the relationship. However, if the two of you are willing to work honestly with each other, you will be able to work through any initial awkwardness to establish a relationship in which you can learn together and about one another—ultimately enabling at least one and quite possibly both of you to be better prepared to serve your organization.

Communicate openly. Probably the most critical aspect of any mentoring relationship is open communication. We believe that mentoring should be a two-way relationship that engages in open, honest sharing. Sometimes such relationships are particularly hard when people are entering cross-race or cross-gender pairings or both at once. If you and your mentor or protégé support true dialogue and are willing to talk and question each other respectfully, we believe you heighten your chances of building a strong mentoring relationship. It is only in this honest, open exploration that the two of you will have the ability to learn the truth of a situation together and figure out an action plan. Go where the options and information lead you.

There is no doubt that being mentored or becoming a mentor can help an individual learn more about himself or herself and the organization. This knowledge is key when one is learning to be politically savvy, a critical business ability for all leaders.

7

Understanding the Political Landscape

Jeremy Dodson could not help noticing the talk in the halls about his managerial choices. As marketing director, he had hired one new manager, an African American woman, Helen Jamison. He had also promoted a black man, Kevin Langston. Jamison had worked in the marketing field for sixteen years, had won three national marketing awards, and her work was fresh and exciting. She was clearly the best candidate of the four Dodson interviewed. Langston had been at the firm for seven years. He was well respected and his work was exemplary. He too had been the best candidate in the field. But the talk in the halls was that Dodson was starting his own little "ghetto fiefdom." Dodson knew that people were talking. A white colleague, Bob Smith, had even come up to him, slapped him on the back, and said, laughing, "So white people aren't good enough for you? It's starting to look like a ghetto down there!"

"I only go for the best," Dodson replied, "and this time I was lucky enough to get them." Though he was not concerned about the quality of his choices, Dodson knew that his credibility and the credibility of those he had hired would be on the line if others believed his decisions were racially motivated. Consequently, he knew he had to manage perceptions if he and his new managers were to have a fair chance at success.

For Jeremy Dodson, as for many others, hiring decisions are political decisions, not because of issues of competence or the attitudes of the candidates but because of race. Indeed, politics and race intertwine throughout the black corporate experience, making the politics encountered by blacks potentially more perilous than the politics experienced by white colleagues—especially white male colleagues. Consequently, being politically savvy is critical for blacks if they are to effectively negotiate the pitfalls that often await them. In *Race, Gender and Rhetoric,* John Fernandez asserts that in addition to racism and sexism, differing personalities, varying leadership styles, limited resources, conflicting goals, and the rapidity of change in the workplace lead inevitably to the need for political shrewdness. It is a factor that cannot be ignored, he concludes, because "politics are the essence of corporate life."

What Political Savvy Looks Like

Within organizations, political savvy is the art of guiding and influencing people's opinions, behaviors, perceptions, and organizational policies. Political savvy is a sensibility: the practical know-how or "street smarts" of corporate culture. Integral to this definition are the concepts of technical and interpersonal competence; self-confidence; and the understanding of people, places, and issues. We believe being politically savvy involves eight distinct yet related activities that people engage in as they try to comprehend work relationships and issues and devise the best ways to manage them. These activities work in harmony to assist leaders in recognizing the dynamic nuances of organizations and in helping them to influence policy, enhance their job effectiveness, and advance their own and others' careers. The eight areas are knowing where you stand and knowing yourself, identifying and understanding power brokers, understanding and maneuvering through organizational currents, garnering appropriate influence, negotiating pitfalls, establishing and maintaining credibility, making meaningful alliances, and effectively negotiating opportunity.

Knowing Where You Stand and Knowing Yourself

A cornerstone of being politically savvy is self-knowledge—intimate knowledge of your own strengths, weaknesses, and motivations. Equipped with accurate self-knowledge, leaders can begin to understand their leverage points and limitations and their potential instruments of influence. Likewise, they can determine their blind spots and areas where they need to grow. Understanding their strengths can give leaders the self-confidence and self-assurance they need to undertake new challenges in the workplace successfully. Such a self-inventory can also help leaders identify strengths or reserves they have that may be useful to the organization.

Not surprisingly, much of how an individual is perceived by others is determined by how that individual conducts herself. Once again Fernandez's research provides insight. Specifically, he advises that knowing yourself and understanding how your culture, strengths, and weaknesses influence your interactions is the first step to solving race and gender challenges. However, he cautions, unresolved race and gender issues held by blacks or others can often hinder an honest and complete self-examination. In situations where racial dynamics may be at play, black leaders must be willing to distinguish between their own issues, the issues of others, and the issues created by the context in which they are operating.

Identifying and Understanding the Power Brokers

In all organizations there are individuals who possess formal or informal power. These are the people who make decisions or who influence those that do. Eileen Bender, a sales manager at a large telecommunications company, describes being challenged as a young, black executive who knew neither the power brokers in her organization nor the way they worked. "Because of the lack of social interaction at the senior management level, I was not sure what politics were at work there. I wasn't even sure if I was on slate for the next level or not. However, my white counterparts seemed to know immediately if they were on track or not for the next level. I didn't know how they knew it. It led me to believe I was seriously missing something." Bender's concerns are like those expressed by many African American professionals who feel left out of the loop. They know that they don't have all the information they need, yet they don't know what they are missing.

Politically savvy leaders know who the power brokers are and the type of power each of these individuals wields. One person's power may be related to a particular topic; another's may arise from technical competence or strong interpersonal ability and charisma. Yet another's power may be determined by proximity to key information or people that makes him a gatekeeper. Of course some people may have power simply because it is vested in their position. Black managers, in particular, have to be clear about where the power in the organization lies if they are to survive both corporate and racial politics. By knowing what power people have and how they use it, politically savvy leaders can take advantage of important leverage points. Such information helps them to more effectively negotiate organizational currents.

Maneuvering Through Organizational Currents

All too often blacks find themselves on the sidelines, acutely aware they are involved in the political "game" yet unsure of the players or rules of engagement. This political ignorance is stifling, for the ability to understand and then skillfully maneuver through workplace currents is critical. These currents are the context in which leadership takes place—they shape how leadership activities will be interpreted and played out. This skill incorporates being circumspect, paying attention to changes or trends on the periphery of organizational consciousness, and formulating an analysis of the current or potential impact of these trends on the organization. A focus on these various waves of activity and influence helps politically savvy leaders recognize and understand the power sources, alliances, and shifts in an organization.

Armed with this insight, politically astute leaders can then chart their course toward desired outcomes, deftly steering clear of organizational "turbulence." The early experiences of Deborah Carter, an oil company manager, underscore the importance and challenge of political maneuvering for African American leaders. Among the most important lessons Carter learned from a white manager were to "play the game" and to pay attention to the periphery. Carter explains that these lessons enabled her to move from being a spectator to being a full-fledged member in the "white corporate world," because they taught her about "knowing the system or how to work within the system to get things done, the kind of relationships you have to build and the support systems, and where to go for information and who to go to for information."

Garnering Appropriate Influence

Beyond understanding and maneuvering through their corporate environments, politically savvy leaders can improve their leverage by garnering appropriate influence. Whether a leader learns to work effectively with and through others or finds methods to extend her influence beyond formal authority, gaining influence is increasingly critical as organizations become flatter and less centralized. In the wake of outdated, ineffective, autocratic management styles, today's leaders are finding new ways to gain clout. These new methodologies are varied and range from increasing technical competence, gaining additional experience in a needed field, and volunteering for additional responsibilities to enhancing interpersonal skills.

For black leaders, increasing their sphere of influence entails additional challenges. The experience of one senior manager we interviewed illustrates this point. "Prior to becoming director of human resources," Danielle Rogers said, "I sought out numerous opportunities to broaden my professional skill and expand my network for the good of my organization. However, my company didn't acknowledge me or realize what they had until I began to gain respect on a

national level through predominantly white human resources professional organizations." Quoting a biblical phrase, she continued,
"a prophet is without honor in his own country," highlighting the
truth that for blacks, just being good may not always be good
enough. Many black managers discover they must wait to be "validated" by superiors and colleagues, even after successfully completing projects or building their reputations outside the organization,
before the internal team will trust and respect their professional
prowess and business acumen. Conversely, at least from their perspective, this "seal of approval" appears to be provided automatically to their white counterparts; it seems a privilege they can lose
rather than one they must earn.

Negotiating Pitfalls

One benefit of understanding the corporate political environment is
gaining the foresight to avoid making mistakes harmful to oneself,
others, or the organization. Once they have a thorough understanding of organizational currents, leaders are better equipped to avoid
or mitigate pitfalls. Each leader's success depends heavily on gathering useful information about potentially difficult situations and then
exercising prudent judgment to use that information appropriately.
Leaders' decisions about whether risks are reasonable can then be
based on the likelihood of success and the context in which they are
being asked to succeed. Negotiating risk also involves knowing
whom to go to and what to do to minimize damage if one is unsuc-
cessful. For blacks, this can be treacherous territory, because even an
honest mistake can set them back or permanently damage their
credibility in the organization. Wilson Davis, a lead technical specialist for a major tobacco firm, provides a vivid analogy: "Living in
corporate America is like being in a river which has an average
depth of about three feet but also has some sinkholes that are twelve
feet deep. We have to be aware of where we are as we walk through
the river of life. . . . We have to be aware of where we are."

Unfortunately, without strong networks, mentors, or other alliances, blacks may find themselves without the benefit of others' knowledge about the location of these sinkholes. Then the supposition that those who don't know history are destined to repeat it plays out again. Davis, however, believes that getting information on how to negotiate pitfalls is a two-way responsibility. "There are some blacks that come to work with the attitude, 'I'm not going to put up with this or that,' or, 'I gave them a piece of my mind.' Well, that's a piece, I tell them, they should have kept to themselves. My father advised, 'When in doubt keep your mouth shut, because a closed mouth gathers no foot.'"

Establishing and Maintaining Credibility

Being politically savvy is not about influence alone. It must be complemented by technical, communicative, administrative, and interpersonal competence. Thus armed, politically savvy individuals can become go-to guys or gals. They can be the people others in the organization consistently count on to get a job done well, correctly, and on time. Discussing an earlier role she held as a human resource technician, Danielle Rogers indicates that although gaining credibility is not easy for blacks, it is certainly within their grasp. Says Rogers, "What helped me earn respect was that my colleagues discovered that regardless of the color of their skin, I supported them. I was fair, I shared information, and I dealt with them as a 'person.' I didn't care about the color of their skin. Soon people came to know that what I said, I had thoroughly considered and thought through. Then instead of going to my boss for advice [the practice in the past when big decisions were to be made], they came to me since I was the company's expert concerning personnel decisions." Although it may be unfair, for black managers, establishing credibility may require exerting additional effort and exercising patience as they seek to assure their colleagues they are both able and eager to do the work for which they were hired. However, part of establishing and maintaining credibility involves being honest about one's strengths and seeking opportunities to improve one's developmental needs. Being open to and soliciting honest feedback can proactively ensure such development.

Making Meaningful Alliances

Gaining an understanding of how to network and with whom to create alliances internal and external to the organization is another aspect of being politically savvy. According to James Sampson, the manager of an Oakland-based recruitment firm, as quoted in an article by S. Branch in *Fortune* magazine, "Too many blacks fail to act strategically early on in their careers by aligning themselves with key players in a company. They get pigeonholed into positions that aren't impacting the bottom line. That's why, when companies merge or downsize, blacks are often the ones asked, 'Do you want to take an early retirement or take a buy-out?' They're the first to get those offers. I've seen it." Not to be confused with friendships, alliances are far more strategic or purposeful and may well be issue based and thus temporary. Consequently, people who have come together to fight for one particular issue may find themselves on opposing sides of the next decision. Such changes in alliance configurations are not unusual. Indeed, debating an issue with colleagues with whom one has recently been aligned on another issue may offer an advantage. The relationship established with these colleagues prior to sitting across the table from them may assist all concerned to find a solution to the current issue that is in the best interests of all parties.

It is also important to recognize that alliances and networks do not have to be limited to people at a higher level than your own. In fact, our personal and training experiences provide overwhelming evidence to the contrary. We work with literally hundreds of executives each year who discover that in addition to their superiors, their peers and direct reports pay close attention to and draw conclusions from their on-the-job behaviors. Some participants learn, to their surprise, that different groups of respondents view their behaviors very differently. Additionally, we find that participants often experience and rate themselves very differently than their colleagues do. Such differences in perception can get in the way of leaders' ability to create and sustain important alliances across organizational lines. If this diversity of perception also holds true in the purposeful relationships they are trying to establish outside of their organization, then leaders must be doubly careful in their interactions with others.

Because African Americans are so often judged by predetermined perceptions rather than reality, they must be particularly aware of the impressions they leave with their coworkers. Aside from accurately determining which groups to align with and for what reasons, leaders must also know when to cut ties and when to stand alone. Decisions to maintain alliances or sever relationships can be crucial. A good understanding and appropriate execution of some of the other activities associated with political savvy can aid leaders in knowing how best to proceed. Leaders should make alliance decisions by considering not who stands the best chance of succeeding but who authentically represents the view they advocate and can advance their position.

Effectively Negotiating Opportunities

Negotiating skills can have a direct impact on whether individuals move up or become derailed in an organization. Critical to developing these skills are interpersonal skills such as listening, understanding other viewpoints, and handling conflicts. A study on derailment conducted by the Center for Creative Leadership and reported on in *The Lessons of Experience* by McCall, Lombardo, and Morrison cites interpersonal skills as crucial for success and the lack of such skills as the main reason people derail in the workplace. Additional CCL research for the multi-rater Benchmarks®

assessment tool (used to measure leader effectiveness) reveals that the superiors, peers, and direct reports of black managers rated them as having better interpersonal skills than their white counterparts. In contrast, the superiors, peers, and direct reports of white leaders believed that they were "quicker studies" and possessed better decision-making skills than their black colleagues. Although there are no data to prove that blacks are indeed more interpersonally effective or that whites are more analytically gifted, there are lessons to be gleaned from these perceptions. Perhaps blacks, of necessity, must showcase their interpersonal skills more often for their business acumen and decision-making abilities to be accepted or appreciated by others. Perhaps whites are more willing to view other whites as quick studies than to see blacks, who have historically been stereotyped as unintelligent, as such.

Not surprisingly, political savvy affects the opportunities that a leader receives. However, these opportunities can be meaningless unless the leader acts on them. All too often leaders fail to take full advantage of opportunities and rob both themselves and their organization of the value that would otherwise be realized. "I don't come to conferences like the National Black MBA Association to party, play, fall in love, or to impress anyone," says Danielle Rogers. "If you don't like me that's okay. I want substance. . . . Don't waste my time—it's valuable and I came here to grow." Making the most of every opportunity is critical to blacks and other nontraditional leaders who may not always believe they receive equal exposure or access to new horizons. Eileen Bender agrees that a large part of negotiating organizational politics is taking advantage of business opportunities. "I've taken advantage of every management development program offered. I've also taken on a couple of six-month assignments—these opportunities forced me to learn quickly and gave me a chance to experience and learn a great deal about other assignments before I got 'married' to them. . . . I could see if it was a good fit or not." Being open to and effectively negotiating opportunities is critical for black managers seeking to expand horizons and gain broader exposure to skills, knowledge, and power brokers.

Why Being Politically Savvy Is Important

Although the notion of playing politics has a dubious connotation, we believe political savvy is an important skill for all leaders and an especially critical one for black leaders. Let us first dismiss the notion that playing the political game is necessarily negative, or even a game at all. Instead, we are inclined to agree with John Fernandez in his assertion that being astute in corporate politics "can become synonymous with the constructive process of finding out how an organization really works; who its powerful and interesting and helpful people are; who really makes decisions; what the true relationships on and off the organizational chart are; where and what the rivalries and factions are; and the like." This is an important realization because so many managers, of all races, deign not to play, attempting to hold themselves above the fray or to keep their heads down so they will not be noticed as political activities take place around them.

What should be evident to everyone is that once people are at work, they are in the political fray. Choosing not to actively participate or develop political savvy means neglecting a tool for proactively advancing one's ideas, topics, projects, and personal career opportunities. As Johnson McDaniel, an African American manager who works for a large chemical company, says, "For God's sake, familiarize yourself early on with the rules of the game, written and unwritten, because they're going to govern behavior, reaction, and attitude."

Although we believe that the eight activities discussed in the previous section are important components of being politically savvy, we admit that few people will be excellent in each. However, we contend there are three areas in which people must excel to be successful. Politically savvy leaders must, first, be aware of and understand the context and culture in which they are being asked to lead. Second, they must also be aware of their own strengths and developmental needs, and third, they must understand their technical and interpersonal competence. With this awareness, leaders have the foundation needed to gain and hone political skills.

Without such a base, leaders lack the context—the knowledge of themselves and their company—to make educated and insightful decisions. They may also lack the competence to gain and maintain professional respect. For black managers, the benefits of being politically savvy are crucial because much of their work takes place in a climate that is ambiguous at best and hostile at worst. For these leaders, understanding themselves, their context, and their culture is not an option but a necessity.

What Is Unique to the Black Experience

Although the benefits and challenges of being politically savvy may be similar in some regards for all leaders, there are additional nuances and features unique to black executives. Race has a way of significantly changing the nature of what to others are simple corporate issues, as well as creating new issues altogether. "Race always influences, especially for a black person. If you don't know that, you have your head stuck in a hole somewhere," says Bob Jackson, a senior project engineer at a major chemical company. "The race issue is always there." Jackson amply summarizes the view that try as they might, blacks must be continually aware of the impact of race in every facet of life, including organizational politics. Although race is not always a critical determinant, to deny its effects is to blatantly ignore an important factor in the political equation.

What do black managers say about office politics? Seventy-two percent of the managers in our study said they believed it was important to engage in office politics (see Figure 7.1). However, even though 79 percent of the managers said they understood the politics of their organizations, only 69 percent believed they handled these politics well. We believe there are a number of reasons for the gap black managers experience between their understanding of and engagement in office politics and their ability to handle these politics adroitly. Specifically, for blacks being politically savvy means being aware of others' perceptions, managing those perceptions by

FIGURE 7.1. Office Politics and African Americans.

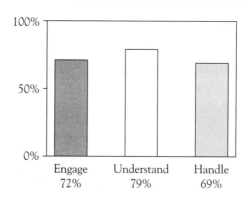

In general, blacks tend to understand politics better than they handle or desire to engage in them.

| | Engage 72% | Understand 79% | Handle 69% |

altering one's own behaviors or by influencing others, and living biculturally with the "disguise" or the metamorphoses that such alterations bring about. Although these survival strategies for African American leaders may enhance their ability to operate within the corporate setting, the very need for their existence may explain, in part, the gap between understanding, handling, and engaging in corporate politics. Many blacks also face additional issues, both benefits and challenges, when working with or for other African Americans. To survive, then, blacks may have to work harder—and continuously. Consequently, in the political arena, they may feel they are leaving things undone or performing poorly, or they may simply just tire of the game.

Being Aware of Perceptions

When they are alert to others' perceptions, African American leaders recognize that they and their white counterparts are often judged by slightly different criteria. In the scenario that opens this chapter, for example, Jeremy Dodson recognized that some of his white colleagues were concerned by his hiring of two African American professionals. Such heightened awareness allows leaders to make decisions and take steps to manage these perceptions. Being ignorant of or unreceptive to such information—and therefore not taking steps to manage others' concerns—can cost leaders like Dodson and his hires their credibility or even their jobs.

Notably, what blacks find frustrating in situations where others' perceptions are mistaken or unfair, and what often contributes to deteriorating trust between blacks and their white colleagues, is the seeming lack of malignant intention behind white colleagues' behavior. Purposeful racism is easier to identify and therefore combat than race-based conjecture. In the scenario about Jeremy Dodson's new hires, Bob Smith did not seem to mean anything derogatory by his "ghetto" comment. Rather, his behavior suggested that he was operating under an unconscious set of assumptions about white advantage. Many blacks would interpret Smith's comments to mean that he *assumed* that Dodson's choices were based on race rather than competency. He *assumed* that having a number of African Americans in one department was not positive. He *assumed* that although there were more whites than blacks in the department, the blacks would have some negative aspects that would overshadow the whites' positive aspects. And he *assumed* that it was his responsibility to drop a hint to Dodson about the potential ramifications of his hiring practices. That is, when Dodson's actions ran counter to Smith's expectations or perceived norms, Smith's reaction may have reflected an unconscious belief that whites should be in the majority and in power rather than conscious racism. The assumptions made on the basis of such beliefs subtly alter the workplace for blacks and other minorities yet the beliefs render these alterations invisible to whites.

Jeremy Dodson's story highlights hiring practices, but the politics of race and their influence on ideas of competency and integrity play out in many other areas as well, including those of firing employees, pursuing contracts, distributing responsibilities, and providing opportunities for employees. As discussed throughout this book, when blacks work with blacks in a white organization, their actions are scrutinized in a way seldom experienced by their white counterparts. For blacks, the burden of having to be hyperaware of their actions and how they will be interpreted can weigh heavily.

Continual vigilance is wearing and can contribute to burnout or, at the least, to the us-versus-them dichotomy that many African Americans experience in the workplace. This "us-them" mind-set encourages African Americans to be wary of their white colleagues' actions, comments, and motives. It undermines mutual trust.

Beyond having constantly to keep one's guard up, such intense scrutiny from white colleagues can make African Americans question their own sense of reality. To be regularly questioned about race and to have few colleagues with whom they can conduct an honest reality check causes some blacks to lose self-confidence. It degrades their entire work environment once they believe that in whites' minds all roads lead back to race. Although some may argue that such questioning is healthy, it is detrimental when it is one-sided. Although African Americans must be careful not to read race as an issue where race does not exist, they also cannot let whites determine where to draw those lines. Because race is not a salient experience for most whites, racial issues often do not register for them. Even when whites are trying to be sensitive, they cannot draw from the same frame of reference as their black colleagues and therefore may be unable to accurately read a situation despite their effort.

As much as being second-guessed, the subtle questioning of an African American leader's principles is often irksome and frankly insulting. To imply that an African American manager will make decisions solely on the basis of race when that leader has shown no other hint of managerial indiscretion is to challenge his or her integrity and credibility.

Managing Others' Perceptions

Once aware of others' perceptions, African Americans often manage them by altering their own behaviors. This does not mean that they bend to others' beliefs or that they succeed in changing others' perceptions. It does mean that they adjust their actions as a way to navigate obstacles and take advantage of opportunities. For example, African Americans may find nonthreatening ways of approaching difficult topics related to race in order to reduce the possibility of misunderstandings. Because race is such a sensitive subject, almost any discussion on the topic is difficult. Blacks who sincerely initiate discussions about race with a mind to listen as well as to share can help put others at ease. Even so, when blacks discuss race, they are often not seen as credible if they are pointing out flaws in the system or racist behaviors. Non-blacks often assume that blacks doing this have ulterior motives or are being hypersensitive; consequently their credibility suffers and their points are often ignored.

Managing others' perceptions, however, often exacts a toll. As discussed in Chapter Four, nine out of ten men in one of our programs said they gave white women performance reviews only with the office door open. Although these men acknowledged that such conversations should be held in private, they felt they had to manage prevailing perceptions about black men and white women, even if the lack of privacy had the potential to skew or restrict open and honest dialogue between professionals. Whether it is the concerns black women have for managing the perception that they are too assertive or the uneasiness black leaders experience when hiring other African Americans, black leaders have to be continually aware of how their actions are perceived because their behaviors are so readily misinterpreted.

Living with a Disguise

At the turn of the twentieth century the poet Paul Laurence Dunbar wrote, "We wear the mask that grins and lies / That hides our face and shades our eyes." Today, more than one hundred years later, many African Americans find these words still ring hauntingly true. Faced with situations in which they must alter their behaviors to manage the perceptions of others, black leaders either become bicultural or adopt a disguise in order to work successfully in corporate America. As discussed in Chapter Two, biculturalism is the ability to comfortably maneuver in one's own culture and in the culture of the work-place, without giving up one's identity. In our study a majority of the black professionals who believed they understood office politics also said they were able to handle the politics well. In addition, these lead-ers responded that aside from wading appropriately through the polit-ical currents, they did not believe they had to give up their identity to be successful; in other words, they view themselves as being suc-cessfully bicultural. To be bicultural is to understand the nuances, challenges, and parameters of both worlds in which one lives—and to be largely accepted in both worlds. In great measure, being bi-cultural is being willing to allow and accept change in oneself as a result of exposure to different views and different experiences.

In our interviews and through our own experiences we have found that the decisions black leaders who are comfortable with bi-culturalism make—the way they look, speak, and act—are all part of political gamesmanship. Other blacks, however, feel these same issues involve their sense of identity and consider such behavioral decisions an intrusion on their lifestyles, one that in effect forces them to adopt a disguise. The line between feeling one's identity is at stake and treating politics as gamesmanship is often blurry and may differ only from the perspective of the person making the deci-sion or facing the issue. Yet the ramifications for both the individ-ual and the organization can be profound. African Americans who feel they are parting with something they consider essential to their sense of self do so at great cost to both themselves and the company. For these employees, the workplace becomes slightly more hostile and foreign. And the company likewise suffers when the imposed, albeit necessary, disguise adopted by these black employees sows seeds of resentment toward and discontent with the organization. Those who view political maneuvering as solely gamesmanship may run the risk of losing their sense of self, individualism, or values. Their organizations may also suffer by having employees who be-lieve the game is all there is. The problem is that these employees may never engage in true interactions.

Black-on-Black Politics

At the same time African Americans are negotiating the political nuances of working with their non-black colleagues, they face an entirely different set of political rules with other black coworkers. A largely undiscussed subject, black-on-black politics is very much alive, well, and prevalent in the workplace.

In some instances this political situation may best be described as a crabs-in-the-barrel syndrome, in which some blacks work to inhibit others from succeeding. This dynamic may spring from the fear some blacks harbor that there is room in the white corporate world for only one successful African American—and they wish to ensure that they are the one and that others know it. A variation on this theme arises when a black leader, perhaps insecure in his blackness, seeks to make examples of other blacks working in the same group. In this scenario, the leader is trying to manage the perceptions of white colleagues by sending the message that he does not treat blacks with special favors. Not only is this behavior unfair and unethical but it serves to infuse chaos and confusion into the workplace and sends the message that blacks are their own worst enemies.

Conversely, there are some African Americans who make life difficult for their black managers by angling for "ye ole hookup"—an unfair or unwarranted advantage. By asking for a "solid" (an advantage or even a guarantee of privilege) and suggesting that "white folks do it all of the time," these employees try to use the race card to get by with inexperience or the performance of inferior work. In most cases the hookup requested is to be given an unearned opportunity, one for which the person has not achieved the requisite level of skill, experience, or education. To be honest, it can be difficult for black managers who truly want to assist other African Americans to turn these colleagues down, for a number of reasons, including a sense of responsibility for the success of others. Some black managers want to make sure they are not setting unfair criteria for African Americans, such as they have witnessed or fallen victim to themselves. Having said this, we argue that at no time is it necessary or desirable for black leaders to carry others or to overlook inferior performance in others simply because they are black. Just as leaders have a responsibility to direct reports to see that they are treated fairly and have opportunities for growth and development, employees have a responsibility to their managers to be competent and perform their jobs at the desired levels set forth for everyone.

A third area of black-on-black politics concerns identity issues. African American leaders may have to deal with black colleagues who use their own racial expectations to determine how these leaders should behave. In short, these leaders do not fit their colleagues' mental models of what a black leader should be—an ideal impossible to meet for everyone because it differs at least somewhat for everyone. Some African Americans do not acknowledge any common bond with other African Americans. Indeed, these folks don't openly acknowledge other African Americans or even their own "blackness." For blacks who embrace their negritude, such attitudes are difficult to understand. A woman in CCL's African-American Leadership Program once described how her black colleague would wait for her to turn a corner before she would step into the hallway herself—apparently so as to not be associated with another black by being in the same hallway at the same time. This example, though extreme, graphically illustrates the extent to which some will go to distance themselves from other African Americans. For whatever reason, these individuals feel they must assimilate completely into the white corporate culture, believing it is detrimental for them to be seen as acknowledging their blackness or identifying with others who are black. Frankly, there is little blacks can do for each other in this situation other than be available for those who distance themselves should they ever decide to reach out to the black community.

Obviously, dealing with black-on-black politics can be trying at times. Fortunately, there is another side to this political coin. Good chemistry between African American colleagues also exists, and when it does it provides those involved with a tremendous resource—a reservoir of support and information and an outlet for frustration. In these circumstances the positive synergy that emerges aids and advances each person's work effectiveness. For example, African American colleagues who talk honestly together can challenge each other's racial perceptions, helping each other determine whether the dynamics of a problematic situation have racial undertones or not. If they decide racial politics are at play, these colleagues can help each other determine the best course of action. Through such conversations, black coworkers may also realize that not everything is about race. Because race is not an issue in these supportive relationships (as it is an area the participants acknowledge having in common), the individuals involved may be able to move into conversations focusing on broader issues. In addition, it is equally clear to us that such positive conversations can also happen across racial lines. However, such discussions and the genuine cross-race relationships that allow them to happen are generally created through a lot of hard work and trust building between participants. When this happens, blacks and others have the opportunity to see each other as rounded individuals, rather than merely racial representatives.

Sometimes being with other African Americans is just "easy"— a safe haven in the storm of daily activities in a white corporate world. Because of their similar experiences, communication and understanding between black colleagues is often simple and clear. For example, most black leaders have had the experience of sitting in a large group meeting with one other black person and hearing a white colleague say something "out of bounds." At that point one of the black leaders looks up, catches the black colleague's eye, and smiles, winks, or subtly nods. They are the only two African Americans in the room, and they *know* without question that they share the same reaction. In that moment they experience a kindred support, knowing that they are not alone but a part of something much larger than themselves.

What You as African American Can Do

To assist African American leaders seeking to enhance their skills in corporate political interactions, we offer the following activities and recommendations. In addition, the Appendix, "Assessing Your Political Savvy," offers a worksheet to help you grow in the critical areas of self-awareness, understanding of your context and culture, and also understanding of your technical and interpersonal competence.

Become aware of the perceptions others have of you. Because it is sometimes difficult to know how others perceive you, it is good to ask for feedback. Select someone whom you trust and who you believe understands the nuances of most political situations. This person may be a mentor, a supervisor, or a peer. Ask him or her to critique your performance in specific incidents where politics were at play. Ask questions such as: How did I do? What was the effect of the point I made? Was I able to capitalize on the moment? Did I use humor effectively? Did my body language and facial expressions increase or decrease my effectiveness? If so, why? How can I improve in these areas?

Inventory your areas of influence. Before you can determine your own areas of influence, it is important to understand the types of influence that have credence in your organization. Harvard professor Linda Hill identifies such categories of influence as inspiration, task, relationship, position, and personal influence. According to Hill, items in these categories can be used like currency, buying their owner influence. Individuals who are strong in the inspirational category may have vision, excellence, or moral and ethical correctness. These individuals may have influence over people who believe these are critical leadership skills. To determine your areas of influence, ask yourself: What are the categories of influence in my organization? What are my strengths and developmental needs in each of the organization's influence currencies? Who or what can help me strengthen my areas of influence? How can I leverage my strengths to become more effective?

Take measured risks. Sometimes African Americans are tagged as being unwilling to take risks. Although this may be the case because, as CCL's Benchmarks studies show, African Americans are also forgiven their mistakes less easily than their white colleagues, risk taking is still an important part of leadership. Taking measured risks includes understanding the context in which you must make decisions and getting stakeholders and power brokers to support your particular decisions or plans of action. These negotiations are best done before making a decision, rather than as cleaning up in the aftermath of a poor decision. So before taking any significant action, conduct a cost-benefit analysis of the potential action. Some questions you may wish to consider are these: What is the action under consideration? What risks are associated with this action? What are the pros and cons of taking this action? Whom will this action significantly affect? How widespread will the effect be? How will people be affected if things go well? If they go poorly? Who are the stakeholders of this action? Who champions the action, and who opposes it? What do I need to do to get more people on board? What will happen if I maintain the status quo?

Another aspect of taking measured risks is establishing and maintaining credibility. If you have a strong track record, people will be more likely to give you the benefit of the doubt when you make a mistake. To evaluate the strength of your credibility, find ways to receive honest feedback from your work colleagues. Use the scales supplied in the Appendix or develop your own items to rate yourself on technical and interpersonal competencies, then ask a trusted colleague (or more than one) to rate you on the same scales and discuss the areas where he agrees with and where he departs from your views. Remember, honesty is essential!

Make meaningful alliances. Part of making meaningful alliances includes being knowledgeable about the coalitions already existing

---

What African Americans Can Do About Politics

Become aware of the perceptions others have of you.

Inventory your areas of influence.

Take measured risks.

Make meaningful alliances.

Make sure your relationships with other blacks are healthy.

---

in your workplace. Make it your business to know others' issues and how their views coincide with yours. One of our interviewees notes that in his organization African Americans are concerned with "justice" and white women are concerned with "equity." Knowing this, he has aligned himself with white women and the power brokers for equity issues and gathered their support for justice issues. When thinking about alliances, consider both whom you can support (direct reports, bosses, peers, and various workplace coalitions) and how you can support them. What do you have to bring to the table? Other questions to ask include: What are the important issues in my workplace? Who are the groups behind these issues? Which issues will benefit me? My department? My project? My coalition? How will these issues benefit me? What influence or leverage do I have with these groups? What issues do we have in common? What will I have to give up to create an alliance with this person or these people?

Make sure your relationships with other blacks are healthy. Several studies suggest that having a good relationship with other African Americans in the workplace helps black managers be more effective. Such relationships can give you emotional support as well as work advice. As you consider your relationships with other blacks, ask yourself these questions: Am I on good terms with them? Do I feel I have to cover for work that is below par? Am I actively trying to undermine any of my coworkers? If so, why? Am I trying to undermine any of my black coworkers? If so, why? What is the benefit of these behaviors, and what is the cost? What do I need to do to help my professional relationships become healthier?

What You as Colleagues Can Do

As the colleague of African Americans and other people of difference, understanding and appreciating how political dynamics affect their workplace experiences is part and parcel of developing your own political savvy. There are insights and alliances to be gained from learning to see the organization through the eyes of others. The Appendix, "Assessing Your Political Savvy," can help you develop awareness of your context and culture and of your interpersonal competence in dealing with issues of race, difference, and power.

Make every effort to avoid misreading situations. All too often, behaviors taken as slights by blacks may not be intended as such. As one of our colleagues often comments, "We judge ourselves by our intentions, while we judge others by their actions." This simple truth should urge individuals to take the initiative to seek out information from those whose actions are in question and to share with them how their behaviors might be misinterpreted. You can also take the time to educate yourself about the challenges faced by black managers and other people of difference to gain a clearer picture of the corporate hurdles they face and the miasma they experience. Reading this book is a great first step. You can also look to other resources such as books (see the References section), corporate training and seminars, and your human resource department.

Become more aware of your assumptions. A critical element in attempting to read situations correctly is to recognize your own preferences, strengths, and developmental issues, which might influence or skew your assumptions about others' behavior. Obviously, people tend to approve and accept behaviors that are similar to their own precisely because they are familiar and therefore easily

What Colleagues Can Do About Politics
Make every effort to avoid misreading situations.
Become more aware of your assumptions.
Maintain equitable expectations.
Make unwritten rules explicit to all members of your team.
Be willing to assist those you deem less savvy.
Be aware of the types and effects of miasma in your organization.
Value diverse perspectives as political assets.

understood. However, when challenged with understanding the behaviors of black leaders, non-black colleagues must ensure they are not jumping to conclusions by stereotyping or making assumptions based on expectations. When considering behaviors with which you are unfamiliar or uncomfortable, before making any conclusions, ask yourself whether these are behaviors that affect performance and success or whether they are simply a cultural or personal expression. If you have trusted agents from whom you can solicit feedback, ask them about the behaviors you are trying to understand.

Maintain equitable expectations. Perhaps the best thing any leader can do is to establish and maintain fair and equitable expectations for blacks, whites, and other colleagues. It is important to recognize that when inequity exists, no matter how subtle, it permeates the entire organization and eventually takes a toll on morale and retention. Additionally, inequity creates conditions in which people are judged differently for the same behavior. Setting reasonable and consistent expectations for every corporate citizen provides realistic goals for them to achieve, giving them an incentive to replicate behaviors desired by the organization. Make sure that all performance expectations are expressed and updated regularly in individual or group discussions and in writing.

Make unwritten rules explicit to all members of your team. In addition to clearly conveying equitable performance expectations for leaders' success, it is also important to communicate the numerous informal expectations—unwritten rules—that all industries and organizations have and that are also critical to leaders' success. To make sure all professionals in your department have access to a level playing field, make it a point to talk to them about the organization's expectations for the attitudes, communication styles, task and team responsibilities, and accomplishments of its leaders. For example, if frequent, open communication is a hallmark of success in your organization, discuss the tactics that potential leaders can develop to meet this standard. At the same time, be sensitive to the reasons why these expectations have developed and ask whether any of them are rooted in assumptions. Also, be sure to convey the various degrees to which the different unwritten rules are important to your organization, so that potential leaders can make conscious, educated decisions about their compliance with these rules.

Be willing to assist those you deem less savvy. Lack of political awareness does not necessarily indicate a lack of desire, professional drive, or intellect. When working with people less politically astute or experienced than you, be willing to view their naivete as an area they can develop, rather than assuming that they are not capable of developing political savvy. If possible, encourage their awareness of political issues by talking about the political impact of the tasks or projects on which they are working or by highlighting the political forces at play in given situations. Increasing the political savvy in your department or among your direct reports can strengthen your relationship to people as well as improve their contributions.

Be aware of the types and effects of miasma in your organization. The political currents discussed in this chapter are those through which your black colleagues and other nontraditional colleagues must work and lead. They are the hidden dynamics affecting the workplace in which you lead too. By paying attention to and understanding the miasma in your organization, you can more effectively develop authentic relationships with black colleagues—whether as a mentor, protégé, ally, or peer. Additionally, you can promote a more productive work environment, one where people can do their best work without being hampered by the burden of difference.

Value diverse perspectives as political assets. Cultivating relationships with African Americans is vital to your own leadership in the increasingly global and fast-paced marketplace. Establishing trusting relationships with nontraditional leaders will give you access to additional, valuable perspectives—and the insights and skills they can bring. Understanding and valuing diverse perspectives can foster more authentic working relationships, provide you with a greater understanding of your organization's internal and external dynamics, and enhance your standing with both traditional and nontraditional colleagues.

Being politically savvy means having an astute understanding of your place in the organization and of the currents that surround you. It means being clear about where others stand in relation to you and the organization. Are these people influencers? Power brokers? Trusted agents? What's more, as an African American, you have to make these judgments as you also work to recognize whether and how race may be affecting the way others perceive you and the way you perceive others and events. Assuming that race is part of every situation is likely to cause you endless grief and numerous misinterpretations of organizational situations. At the same time, ignoring race when it is a factor in events is naive and foolish. Striking the balance between these two extremes is a necessary political skill if you are to succeed in corporate America. We suggest you use your trusted agents to help you correctly read your organizational climate—racial and nonracial. Beyond understanding your environment, you must be prepared to act on the insights such knowledge brings and to be responsible for the actions you take.

PART TWO

Coming Together

In Part One we discussed many aspects of miasma that influence the environment in which African Americans work and lead. These characteristics are dynamic, creating infinite combinations and making the miasma that each individual encounters unique to that person. Yet even though miasma is dynamic—its consistency constantly changing as it swirls around African Americans and other people of difference—individual and corporate responses have not always been as active. A common response by people of all colors is to put their guard up and keep their heads down as they plow through daily interactions. "Keep it shallow and keep it moving" is the motto of many colleagues who talk openly about work but shy away from any conversations that involve race, trust, and interdependency and the ways these factors affect the workplace. Many organizations function in a similar manner, offering well-meaning diversity initiatives that are too simplistic to deal with the enormous psychosocial complexities of these issues. Other organizations do not address diversity issues at all, for a variety of reasons. Whether that is because they assume all their leaders operate in the same context or because they believe "the less said is the best said," or whether they have any number of other explanations, the fact is that organizational failure to acknowledge and address diversity concerns can degrade individual, team, and organizational effectiveness.

Given the current state of affairs, we believe there are opportunities for blacks, their colleagues, and organizations to improve and enhance the dynamics of corporate life. Hence the final three chapters of this book are dedicated to exploring recommendations and guidelines. We do not presume to have all the answers to all the issues that concern black leaders. Rather we hope to provide a starting place, some practical suggestions and food for thought. We have created and compiled these guidelines on the premise that the only person in whom you can bring about change is yourself. Moreover, because this book is dedicated to detailing the corporate experiences of African American leaders, it should be no surprise that the guidelines offered to black executives are more extensive than those provided for colleagues and organizations. Our research, coupled with our own experience as black professionals, has provided us with a rich storehouse of recommendations and strategies for African Americans who are striving to improve their leadership journey. Additionally, it is our intention and hope that the suggestions provided for black leaders' colleagues and organizations will serve as a springboard, initiating deeper discussions and increasing opportunities for the full engagement and incorporation of black professionals.

Seeing diversity issues as belonging only to blacks or other nontraditional corporate citizens will ensure that little or no change will occur around corporate diversity issues. Conversely, if organizations and leaders recognize that everyone has a stake in this issue, and as such it belongs to everyone, our society has a better opportunity to move forward. To help all stakeholders consider and accept these issues of difference and how they can be improved, this section devotes a chapter to each key group. Chapter Eight reviews what blacks can do to improve their workplace situation. Chapter Nine discusses what others can do to improve perceptions, communications, and equity in the workplace. And Chapter Ten explores what organizations can do to systemically address or neutralize the miasma of difference.

The recommendations in these last three chapters differ from the advice offered to African Americans and their colleagues at the end of each chapter in Part One. Specifically, while Chapters Two through Seven provide pointed advice about working through each of the six areas that are different for the African American executive, the final three chapters provide a more general approach to address the larger condition of miasma. These chapters provide readers with guidelines that help the African American executive and his or her colleagues both recognize and deal effectively with the intangible and tangible effects of difference in the workplace.

Some constant themes run through the recommendations offered in these chapters. In essence, we believe that for individuals to successfully improve their interpersonal relationships and organizational effectiveness, they must, first, gain greater insight into their actual and potential strengths and developmental needs. Second, they must engage in self-education about others and the workplace environment to determine where it might be necessary to make adjustments or think differently about colleagues or the workplace. Thus educated and armed with behavioral skills and goals, leaders can begin working on making the organization work more effectively and equitably.

8

Strategies for Black Managers

As African Americans attempt to confront the issues of miasma that surround them at work, it is important to recognize that they must bear some responsibility for resolving these issues. Although we certainly do not intend to blame the victims of miasma or suggest that only blacks carry the onus for correcting the situation, we do suggest that the workplace challenges around difference are complex. Although African Americans have not initially caused these challenges, they may now be contributing to them. Therefore, if blacks really wish change to occur, they need to recognize ways in which they might be contributing to the discomfort of their own existence. They may need to consider how they may be limiting themselves and their view of the world or how their perceptions may cause them to misinterpret others' intentions. In some situations, blacks may need to act as the catalyst for change in individuals, teams, or the larger organization. Frankly, because they are the people feeling pain, they may have greater motivation and more sense of urgency than others to see that these problems get resolved. Those who are comfortable have little incentive to change the status quo.

As you read the suggestions and strategies that follow, you will certainly find many things you already do. We invite you to skim through those sections. In other sections you may find new ideas, lessons, or behaviors you will want to consider adopting to help you enhance your leadership potential. Because the issues leaders have to deal with are so varied, we have not attempted to provide point-by-point action plans for addressing specific situations. Inevitably, we would leave scenarios or problems unexplored. Instead, we encourage you to use the following guidelines as prompts to develop new strategies appropriate to you as an African American leader in corporate America. Once you get in the habit of thinking consciously, comprehensively, and constructively, then you will always have a way to attack situations regardless of the specifics.

Self-Development

You can be the single greatest force and asset to your success. It is unlikely that much corporate growth will take place if you do not look first to yourself to see how and where you can improve. Sometimes people find it easier to see what others are doing to them than to see what they are doing to (or not for) themselves. The first step in self-development is to see yourself as having both power and agency—the capabilities to make your situation better. Self-development goes a long way in helping people feel secure in their leadership abilities.

Know yourself. Knowing yourself can be the best foundation for leadership. Having an awareness of your talents, developmental needs, values, beliefs, and dreams can help you define who you are. This self-definition is important, particularly for African Americans, because so many others are willing to define you and, potentially, to define you negatively. If you are not sure of yourself, you can unconsciously fall into believing others' perceptions of you. So make sure you know yourself better than anybody else does. Know your personal vision: who you are, what you believe in, where you are starting from, what resources you can draw on, and where you want to go. Be clear about your strengths and weaknesses, and be conscious of the responsibilities you are willing to shoulder.

Self-Development

Know yourself.

Stretch your comfort zone.

Focus on your goals.

Be hungry for knowledge.

Knowing and being comfortable with yourself allows you to lead from a position of strength. Such comfort also gives you the chance to explore new ideas and grow as a person, not just because someone is expecting you to but because you want to expand your own horizons. Knowing yourself is perhaps the best defense you can develop against the many complications and obstacles that face African American leaders in the workplace. You can gain additional self-knowledge from formal development programs or assessment tools that measure your preferences, your styles, and others' perceptions about your abilities and impact. You can also learn from taking time for self-reflection. In this process you might ask yourself such questions as: What do I value about my work? What am I willing to do and not do to be successful? How much am I willing to put up with in this or any organization? Such questions help you define the parameters in which you are willing to work—they help you define your personal boundaries.

Stretch your comfort zone. Today's employment environment does not make room for employees who do not continue to learn. Stretching your comfort zone can prevent stagnation. By expanding your knowledge and experiences, you broaden your acceptance and respect for people and practices that are different. This in turn can enhance your business acumen and ability to develop and nurture professional relationships. If pushing your boundaries to try new things is a frightening concept, go slowly at first. You can begin by engaging in new behaviors, relationships, or attitudes that are fairly safe. Then as you become comfortable with these activities, try something a little riskier. Put your name in for that job you have always wanted. Or approach someone whom you would like to get to know better, a potential mentor perhaps. The areas that define your comfort zone and where you need to stretch will depend upon your personal situation.

Focus on your goals. Career management is an individual responsibility. You cannot rely on someone else to do it for you. As one of our colleagues, David Campbell, advises in his book *If You Don't Know Where You're Going, You'll Probably End Up Somewhere Else,* leaders should be clear about their professional direction. Consider what it will take to get you to your desired destinations. Be proactive in networking and seek mentors who can help you increase your leadership effectiveness. Look at the other people in your organization, particularly African Americans and other nontraditional leaders if there are any, and determine what has or has not been helpful in their careers. What lessons from their careers can you adapt for your own situation? Be cautious about developing your career at the whims of other people. This is your life, your career, so be proactive—take charge of your own destiny. Things that may hinder or distract you from reaching your goals successfully include allowing your ego to get in the way of a realistic appraisal of your abilities; failing to attain appropriate, requisite skills to do the job; lacking commitment; or losing sight of your goals by pursuing ill-conceived alternatives. Of course it is always important to periodically reevaluate your goals in light of your current desires and experiences. Whether your original goals are still valid or you are working from a revised plan, it is crucial that you know what your goals are to help you productively focus your energies and abilities.

Be hungry for knowledge. You should be more than just curious about your job and your industry. Instead, be hungry for knowledge that spans areas beyond your industry and expands into your other interests or issues peripheral to your industry. As you gain additional specific and general knowledge about your field you are more likely to see trends, understand nuances, and determine patterns. As businesses become more complex through changing technology, globalization, and increasing diversity, the more understanding your context and keeping yourself updated becomes critical to your personal and organizational success. Ask questions, read, and begin to understand not only what your job calls for but why it calls for these things. Get a clear understanding of your advancement possibilities and what you may need to do to grow so those possibilities come to pass. Do not be overly concerned about moving into another role or organization while you still have learning and growth opportunities in your current position. But if an opportunity comes along for which you believe you are qualified, give it ample consideration.

Education

In working to become more effective leaders, African Americans will benefit from educating themselves more fully about themselves, others, and their environment. By purposefully gaining knowledge, they can broaden their perspective about themselves and the world around them. This broader perspective will help them become more effective and strategic leaders by providing opportunities to see and understand beyond their own sphere.

Learn about others and their miasma. To learn more about the other cultures represented in your workplace, read about, talk with, and observe those with whom you work. Pay attention to how different people around you negotiate the workplace and how others perceive and react to them. Be careful not to assume that you know or understand everything about whites or other groups or that other nontraditional groups are unimportant to you. By learning more about others, you can gain greater understanding of the reasons that people behave as they do. Such knowledge can help you more accurately interpret your environment and the events that occur in it.

You may also discover more similarities than you expect. Other racial and ethnic minorities, as well as other groups such as homosexuals and women, also face discriminatory practices or less-than-welcoming attitudes in the corporate world. Recognize that these groups have their own stories and sets of challenges. This can help ensure you do not become so caught up in what has been done to blacks that you lose sight of the difficulties that others experience. Watch out for the "Who's the most oppressed?" competition; such conflicts between groups are disabling and destructive. As Johnson McDaniel, a manager at a major chemical company, says, "Learn to become more familiar with [other groups'] agenda, to see the issues they're going through and they're going for."

Understand others' expectations of you. Part of being a black leader means contending with the various expectations others may have of you. First, you need to know what these expectations are and why someone or some group has invested you with them. To do this, you may need to diplomatically ask about the *whats* and *whys* surrounding others' plans for you. Their answers may give you some insight into the miasma that you contend with every day. Thus armed, you can decide whether you agree with these expectations and whether you are willing to take on others' beliefs about what you should do. Too often, black leaders feel weighed down by others' expectations, yet feel they must live up to them anyway. We believe it is important to remember that you can choose to accept, accept in part, or reject others' expectations. Your decision-making process should be partly informed by how you feel about that expectation. What will it mean to you to give up an expectation or to strive to meet it? Is that cost one you are willing to pay? We are not suggesting that you go through life selfishly ignoring others, but we do think that each of us is entitled to live the life we wish for rather than the life others want for us.

Seek out feedback. As an African American leader, you cannot afford to be uninformed about how people see you or your work.

Education

Learn about others and their miasma.

Understand others' expectations of you.

Seek out feedback.

Determine and expand your areas of influence.

Be aware of your assumptions and expectations.

Expand your ideas about identity.

Understand your context.

Don't be naive about racism.

Learn when to leave.

The benefit of the doubt some people are willing to give you is often not as expansive as it is for others, and the band of acceptable behavior some people see for you may not be as wide as it is for others. Thus it becomes important for you to have a strong and accurate sense of how you are perceived in terms of personal interaction and job performance. With this knowledge, if you have to make corrections, you may be able to do so in midcourse when they are still minor ones, rather than facing major corrections later.

To get accurate feedback about your behaviors and how others perceive them, you might engage a trusted friend or mentor to help you (as discussed in Chapters Four and Six). You might also seek to enhance communication with your direct reports, encouraging them to give you feedback as well as your providing feedback to them. Likewise you can ask your supervisor for regular feedback throughout the year rather than just during your annual appraisal period. A more formal way to gather feedback is to use a multi-rater instrument that allows a variety of people in the workplace to provide you with feedback (in some cases anonymously) regarding their perception of your performance or behaviors. Some instruments to consider are Benchmarks®, 360 BY DESIGN℠,

SKILLSCOPE®, and Prospector® (all of which are Center for Creative Leadership tools). Please note that many multi-rater assessments must be administered by a certified facilitator, who then assists you in interpreting your feedback accurately. Regardless of the methods you use, gathering feedback should become a regular part of your managerial routine.

Determine and expand your areas of influence. As you obtain information about how you may be perceived, you can begin to develop a more accurate understanding of your areas of influence. You can gain insight into where you are strong, where you have engendered trust, and where you have established credibility—all of which can help you to see if there is a theme on which you can build further. Make note of the areas in which people seek out your expertise and those in which they don't. Keep track of the subject area discussions in which you are included and from which you are excluded. Observe how often your suggestions are taken, incorporated into a final decision, or not considered. If you find you are not as influential as you believe you should be, there are some strategies you can follow to help change that situation.

First, be sure that you have the requisite expertise (or at the very least are skilled) in the relevant subject areas. Continuous learning and skill development can be crucial in helping you gain and maintain the desired knowledge. As your expertise grows, so should your area of influence. Second, you may have to ask yourself, and your trusted agents, if personality issues or interpersonal behaviors are limiting your sphere of influence. Third, you might want to check in with colleagues who have not used your input to determine if and why you may have been overlooked. If you truly believe you are amply qualified yet not fully influential, then you may have to spend some time in establishing or building credibility with your colleagues. This may mean stretching your comfort zone by sharing expertise, information, or desires for being brought into conversations and decisions as appropriate. If after considerable effort you make no progress in expanding your influence, you may need to consider moving on. Once you have a clear sense of your capabilities, determining your appropriate levels of influence can reduce guesswork. In some cases this may mean acknowledging that you are not yet qualified to exert influence in some of the areas where you want to be a player.

Be aware of your assumptions and expectations. Although others' assumptions and expectations may be troublesome to you, your own can also be quite a burden if left unexamined. What assumptions do you bring to the table, and whom are they about? Are they accurate? For example, if you assume that other blacks in the office are intent on bringing you down in the organization, on what is this belief founded? It may be as untrue as the assumption that they are all there to help you. If you expect that your organization will fail to consider you for a particular role, on what is that belief based? Again, you may be wrong. Be aware of the ways in which your assumptions and expectations may constrain or help you. If, for example, you expect excellence from yourself regardless of others' expectations, you will be more likely to succeed than if you allow yourself to be limited by others' thoughts.

Expand your ideas about identity. For an African American in the workplace, identity issues are never far away. It is important to decide what identity means to you so that you are not buffeted by conflicting notions of identity from the company, other blacks, and other people in general. Many blacks have to determine how much of themselves they are willing to give up in the workplace and in what ways they can express themselves in that environment without compromising their identity or jeopardizing their credibility. We encourage you to determine what personal cost you are willing to pay to keep, lose, or express your identity. Remember that identity issues and expressions are different for each individual. As a consequence it is not only difficult but unfair to make judgments about others' identity decisions.

Although it is important to determine what identity means to you, we also suggest that you allow your ideas about identity to grow.

Use your opportunities as a leader to expand notions of identity for yourself and about others. If you are truly clear about who you are, engaging in new experiences and challenging or expanding your concept of identity will not change your basic identity. In fact it can strengthen your self-concept, enabling you to become more multi-cultural and giving you a better opportunity to understand and interact with others. In addition, expanding your ideas on identity can reduce limitations you might have put on yourself and others. Such an opening up of ideas may lead to greater insights into your relationships with people who don't behave exactly as you think they should.

Understand your context. Familiarize yourself with the written and unwritten rules of your organization, and use that information to govern your attitude, behaviors, and reactions. Because as an African American you may not have the same networks and information conduits as many of your colleagues, you may have to rely more on yourself than others. With an understanding of the context in which you are working, you are more likely to correctly anticipate and interpret what is going on around you. Anna Dutch, senior executive for a professional sports team, says developing this skill takes patience. "You have to know your boss and the people you work for," she said. "Know their philosophy. Get into their brains and think what they think. Knowing the people you work for helps you to maneuver a lot easier." To learn about an environment, ask questions of your trusted agents and mentors about the organization's dynamics. Predict how you believe people will behave in given situations and then watch how they in fact behave. Be aware of events that are happening beyond your specific area of responsibility. In order to increase your organizational awareness, also read company newsletters, familiarize yourself with the organization's intranet, and simply listen to the rumblings around the watercooler.

Don't be naive about racism. Although we don't believe there is a racist lurking around every corner, it would be naive to think that racism doesn't exist in some workplaces. There are many people who have conscious or unconscious racist notions and many organizations that have subtle racist practices. Although these beliefs and practices are rarely overtly articulated, they can subtly affect how African Americans are judged and the opportunities they receive. That this is so should not be surprising. Racism in the United States is not a new phenomenon. Certainly, knowing and understanding your work context can help you determine strategies for going forward. Such strategies might include being circumspect in new situations and documenting events that have a racial undertone in case you are challenged on your behaviors at a later period. Whether you are involved in personnel issues, business practices, operational decisions, or interpersonal relationships that involve race, be cognizant of the impressions that can be drawn from your behaviors and decisions.

Learn when to leave. Determining when to leave an organization can be trying. Many African Americans, feeling underutilized in one organization, will pack their bags and move to another. However, because many organizations underutilize blacks, moving aimlessly from one place to another searching for respect may prove fruitless. If you are considering a move, first ask yourself whether you have learned all there is to learn at your present institution. Honestly consider whether you have been proactive in seeking opportunities and information there. Have you taken advantage of all the company has to offer you? Have you asked for developmental opportunities? Have you asked to be assigned to another department if you believe you are being underutilized? Is it unlikely the situation will change? Have you checked you own attitude and your own ability to contribute at a higher level? Have you allowed yourself to stay in one place long enough to have had the opportunity to excel? It may be that you have to make your stand at your current institution to learn how to survive in corporate America. Once that lesson is learned, you might consider staying even if another company offers an attractive package.

However, you may decide to leave your organization if you believe you have exhausted every opportunity to grow, to improve your contributions, and to get others to acknowledge your efforts and better employ you. Although patience and persistence are important, there is little value in constantly beating your head against a wall. That simply hurts.

Behavior

To become more valuable leaders, African Americans may need to go beyond educating themselves to employing behaviors that can increase their effectiveness and credibility. Although it is clear that many of the issues and situations blocking their success are externally created, there remain many areas over which they have some control. In some of these areas they may be limiting their own effectiveness without realizing it. In other areas they may simply need to expand their repertoire of behaviors to create a wider range of options and opportunities.

As leaders, people face added pressures, visibility, and responsibilities but have potentially greater leverage to accomplish things. How leaders interact with others is key to their ability to lead effectively—to put people at ease and to get things done. Presentation and carriage—how people handle themselves every day at work—is but one influential aspect of interaction. Because African American leaders physically stand out in their organizations and because they believe they are being constantly judged, it is important they be aware of how they present themselves. Your presentation and carriage is largely about how you create and manage others' perceptions of you.

Be prepared when communicating. Whether addressing groups or individuals, in formal or informal conversations, never assume that people automatically understand you or the point you are trying to make. Present your facts and your rationale so that others can follow your reasoning (for example, use the "language" they speak and

Behavior
Be prepared when communicating.
Listen.
Use appropriate language.
Balance assertiveness with approachability.
Be yourself.
Be a change agent.
Demand and enforce equitable treatment.
Support the vision of the organization.
Remember, you don't have to have all the answers.
Be deliberate in your actions.
Don't be preoccupied with racism.
Bring something to the table.
Be patient, prepared, and persistent.
Sharpen coping skills.

employ methods with which they are familiar, whether metaphors, spreadsheets, diagrams, or pie charts). This practice helps your supporters to understand your viewpoint and allows you to demonstrate to any detractors that you have done your homework. It is also wise to anticipate some of the various scenarios that might occur when you are communicating so that you can have a considered response prepared. And finally, don't hesitate to speak up in a meeting as long as your comments add value. Presenting a different viewpoint for consideration, asking a pointed question, outlining areas of weakness, or elaborating on the issue at hand can add to the discussion and contribute to your visibility.

Listen. Because understanding your context and those around you is so critical to your survival, it is important to *actively* listen to what is being said. Beyond the fact that listening is simply a good communication and leadership skill, listening is likely to yield a great deal of information about the people, projects, and issues around you. Additionally, effective listening enables leaders to gain clarity and agreement on the issues at hand. It is an error to believe that communication consists only of talking. Though listening is the lesser used skill, it is probably more important. To be an engaged listener, do not think ahead or focus on what your response should be, but concentrate on the speaker and the points being made. Take time to absorb and consider what is being said. Ask thoughtful questions for clarification or repeat back to people what you have heard. Use phrases such as, "I'm hearing you say . . ." or, "Am I correct in understanding that . . ." to confirm and acknowledge others' viewpoints. Trust that your opinions and responses will be stronger with the complete understanding that comes from active listening.

Use appropriate language. Let's be honest, people are just waiting for black folk and other non-whites to make grammatical errors or use slang in the business setting. Although many whites routinely slaughter the English language, unless they come from obviously rural backgrounds their misuse of the language is not usually perceived as a lack of intelligence. This benefit of the doubt does not extend to African Americans. Some people assume blacks' native language is Ebonics (the vernacular some blacks use in social settings) if they make a grammatical mistake or lapse into slang at a moment that calls for standard English. Ironically, the same people who think this are usually themselves users of industry jargon or other terminology that serves as conceptual shorthand.

Consider the language of your workplace and monitor your own language to see how you express yourself at work. Get feedback about your grammar from those you can trust if you believe it may not be standard, then make moves to correct your language if that is needed. Realize too that Ebonics is not "bad," it is simply not the language of the workplace. Here is an area where it pays to be bicultural, to be able to move between languages. Equally as important as enhancing your verbal skills is enhancing your written skills. There are very few jobs today that do not require writing ability. Whether the materials you need to produce are reports, business plans, or memos, your ability to craft a succinct, well-written document is vital to establishing and maintaining your credibility. This is not about giving up your identity; it is simply about learning the style of professional communication and the jargon of your industry.

Balance assertiveness with approachability. Be assertive and confident as you go about your daily business. However, understand that for African Americans such behaviors may be interpreted as pushy or threatening. Although we do not suggest that you become less assertive, we do suggest that you adopt behaviors that help to manage others' perceptions of you. Use behaviors that make you approachable, such as having a firm but not crushing handshake. Keep your countenance pleasant, because people tend to assume they can tell others' moods and attitudes from facial expressions. Cultivate ways to make small talk. This does not mean we are suggesting you take up a Stepin Fetchit routine. Being sociable is not a white thing, nor is it "kissing up" to people. It is a way of carrying yourself so that others want to get to know you and can do so easily.

Be yourself. When you are comfortable and authentic with yourself, you are more likely to lead from a position of strength. Focus on behaving in ways that are authentic and comfortable to you. You do not have to justify who you are to anyone, least of all yourself. Being authentic, in turn, will help you appreciate the diversity you bring to the table. It should also help you to appreciate and not be threatened by the difference in style or opinion that others bring to the table. As Walter Max, a special projects manager, advises, "So just kind of be yourself, and try to focus on what you are comfortable with, and your own identity." Max says people should "use that comfort to their own advantage rather than feeling as if they have to transform themselves into something that they're not." Logically, as people increase their trustworthiness as perceived by others, they increase their personal comfort level; they decrease the stress and strain that comes from having to hide their true selves; and they gain access to the wisdom they've acquired in other aspects of their lives for use in the professional arena.

Be a change agent.   Use your status as someone who is different to become an agent of change. Candice Casey, team leader of a national financial company, says she uses the fact that many of her colleagues see her as outside the mainstream to her own benefit. "They don't view me as part of the mainstream, so it allows me the opportunity to bring something that might be unusual or different." By honing her different perspective and effectively verbalizing her thoughts, Casey is able to turn what might have been a disadvantage to an advantage. Being a change agent might entail suggesting new ideas or different perspectives, challenging the status quo, or volunteering to spearhead change projects. Keep in mind, though, that if you are going to be an effective change agent, you need to have established strong credibility. Also remember, trust and accomplishment are requisites for garnering credibility.

Demand and enforce equitable treatment.   You have the right to be treated equitably in your workplace. If you feel that is not happening, check your perceptions with others, document the different treatment, and then take your concerns to the appropriate company personnel (such as your supervisor, the HR staff, or an executive you can trust). If after you seek help your issue is not adequately addressed within the organization, you may have to go outside for help or guidance. This may include taking your concerns to government oversight agencies, private "watchdog" groups, the media, or even an attorney. It would be naive to assume that just because you report inequitable treatment people will appreciate the news. It is not uncommon for people who point out work problems to be plateaued or even fired. Yet there are many others who as a result of speaking out get their situation corrected. Some even get restitution. It is not always easy to determine how your organization will behave, unless you are able to judge its reactions by past history. Make sure you have thought through the potential consequences of reporting poor treatment. Decide if it would be better for you to leave or to stay and fight. The fact is no one has to accept inequitable treatment from any individual or any organization.

When you are in charge, make sure that you set equal standards and enforce equitable treatment for everyone in your sphere of influence. Such treatment should be equitable not only for blacks and whites but for all in the workplace, whatever their differences in ethnicity, age, sexual orientation, nationality, religion, and so forth. The bottom line is that blacks cannot demand equitable treatment for themselves if they do not demand it for others as well.

Support the vision of the organization. As an organizational leader, you need to publicly support the organization's vision, mission, and the decisions or direction of your superiors. This does not mean that you have to agree with every decision made or the overall strategy, but after you have adequately and appropriately expressed your disagreement, you should be able to communicate the decision to your staff without seeming disingenuous. This task may be particularly difficult when you feel the company is dealing poorly with diversity issues. If you find yourself in a situation where you truly cannot support the vision, mission, or organizational decisions, you may have to make some tough decisions of your own.

Remember, you don't have to have all the answers. Many leaders feel that to be considered effective leaders they need to have all the answers. Black managers in particular take on this burden, fearing that if they do not have all the answers, people will view them as incompetent. The fact is that no one has all the answers—and you shouldn't pretend as if you do. Such pretense is more likely to end badly than well. Instead, let your staff know that you value their input and contributions and that you are invested in their personal growth. Find ways to work on problems together. Being a good leader sometimes means facilitating the discovery of the right solution or stepping back and allowing your team members the freedom to find their own answers. By stepping back you can increase your team's respect for you while engendering team members' trust and fostering their development.

Be deliberate in your actions. When you present yourself to the workplace, be very conscious of the actions you are taking. There is considerable evidence to suggest that African Americans and others of difference are more individually visible than their mainstream colleagues. Consequently, it is important to be mindful of how you conduct your corporate business. As Johnson McDaniel recommends, "pick your battles, pick your friends, and pick your people." Although you cannot direct all the events that take place around you, you can at least exercise control over selected elements. Such control helps you determine how you will use your influence and with whom. Being deliberate in your behaviors involves considering consequences before acting and declining to waste time on things that don't mean much to you or the organization. You may also wish to be careful about where and when you show your vulnerabilities or vent your frustrations. And very important, do not threaten to do anything unless you fully intend to follow through. Threatening an action then turning away from it at the time when you should be following through diminishes your credibility, unless you can justify the change of heart.

Don't be preoccupied with racism. Racism exists. That's a fact. However, your being preoccupied with racism—or the fact that there are two sets of rules—will not cause racists to lose a moment's sleep. What will disturb their peaceful slumber, though, is your success. Your determination to excel, in spite of racial barriers, can armor you against unfair onslaughts in the corporate arena. Decide what adjustments you need to make or rules you need to challenge to further your objectives. Remember, success truly is the best revenge. So, stay focused on the goal. Be prepared for setbacks, and find ways to learn from them. These lessons may help you improve your skills or they may give you fresh insights into an individual's or organization's workings. By beating yourself up and getting bogged down in the injustice, you only let "them" win. Rather than spending an inordinate amount of your time focusing on racism, we suggest you identify unfair practices to appropriate agencies and let them deal with the situation. Trust in the system until the system proves untrustworthy. In doing so, you will be freer to devote your energies to more productive endeavors.

Bring something to the table. Getting hung up over what is fair and what is not will not bring you success in corporate America. Everyone can agree that the business world is not fair. Most will even admit that it is not fair to African Americans and others of difference. However, once that admission is made, blacks are no better off than they were before. Instead, they have to "bring something to get something." They have to be willing to work and to work hard. They cannot be known only for their complaints but also have to be known for their excellence. This may sound as if we are asking you to subscribe to the notion that blacks have to work twice as hard as their white male counterparts. We aren't! Instead, we are simply stating that you have to add value to the organization and be perceived as doing so. So, let your work, attitude, and behaviors speak for you. Demonstrate through your actions that you want to be successful. Remember, it's not about you, it's about the job.

Be patient, prepared, and persistent. Bide your time in the workplace. As David Thomas and John Gabarro in their book *Breaking Through* show, people of color are not playing the same game as their white colleagues. This may mean that you have to learn to be patient, particularly when you first start out. But being patient is not the same as being inactive. While you are waiting, prepare yourself. Learn all that you can learn from your job. Make your presence and your curiosity felt as you wait for your time to shine. Again, we are not suggesting that you become reactive in your career. Rather, when you are prepared, let the right people know that you are interested in new or different opportunities. Be persistent, not annoying, in your pursuit of these opportunities. If you are not given a chance, ask those in charge why you have not received the opportunity and let them know that you still want to be considered for other jobs. If you are given specific feedback about why you did not get a particular job, evaluate it with an open mind, then work to hone the skills or knowledge areas that were missing, and then try again.

Sharpen coping skills. Stuff happens. And frankly, it often happens at the most inconvenient moments. Sometimes, getting through sticky issues is more a matter of survival and resilience than skill. Robert Simpson, an account executive at a metropolitan utility company, remembers his mentor advising him to "cover up, weather it, wipe yourself off when it happens, and keep on rolling." Inherent in this view is the understanding that much of what happens at work is not personal. Some things happen to you because you are black, other things "just because"—the salient question is, how are you going to handle them? If you see everything as a personal attack, you lose objectivity and eventually credibility. A more effective and healthy approach is to wait until the situation quits hitting the fan, and then assess your options. Determine the probable cause of the situation to see whether it is likely to happen again. Develop a plan of action for mitigating the current circumstances and for improving or getting rid of the problem. All these strategies can be more effectively accomplished with the assistance of others with whom you can openly explore ideas and from whom you can solicit honest feedback. These informal consultants—mentors, trusted agents, family, friends, or other colleagues—can help you see how you handle situations and provide useful insights for sharpening your coping skills. Face it—trying times affect even "good" people, and they generally happen more than once. Improving your coping skills will develop your resiliency, provide you with opportunities for growth, and better prepare you for the next hardship or challenge.

Building Relationships

Being adept at developing and maintaining strong interpersonal relationships is an important leadership capability. For African Americans having strong interpersonal skills is especially crucial. Effective relationships are your foundation for successfully negotiating the work environment. Unless you have the ability to form truly symbiotic relationships, people may limit their interactions with you to areas where they believe you have validity. Unfortunately for African Americans, that validity is often reduced to matters of race. However, blacks may often limit their interpersonal effectiveness by opting to operate in a professional yet distant manner. The strategies that follow talk about ways in which you can engage, expand, and enhance your relationships. We challenge you to discover how you can make your interactions with your colleagues richer and more meaningful, personally and professionally.

Find ways to bridge the gap. For some African Americans the distance between themselves and their non-black colleagues may seem like a chasm. For other blacks that distance may seem merely a hand's breadth. Often the difference between these two viewpoints resides only in the minds of the individuals, who have varying degrees of willingness, skills, and optimism for bridging this gap. At the same time, there is another dynamic at work, which manifests itself in the willingness, skill, and optimism that non-black colleagues bring to the relationship. The perceived distances—whether large or small—affect whether, how, and to what degree people are willing to engage in more than pseudopersonal relationships. Bridging these interpersonal divides enables people to see one another more clearly, enhances communication, and provides greater opportunities for connection with others. To engage in this manner means to move beyond superficial involvement with colleagues and establish genuine, open, mutually beneficial relationships—both personally and professionally. For blacks, this can be a multifaceted challenge, because they are dealing not only with their own mind-sets and behaviors but also the mind-sets and behaviors of others.

Although you cannot control the behaviors of others, there are strategies you can employ to bridge the gap. First, take a mental survey to determine the extent of your interpersonal distance from colleagues. Second, attempt to ascertain the reasons these various gaps exist and the things you might do to affect these reasons. Next, decide whether closing these gaps is worthwhile for you, and which gaps you deem most important to close. Determine if the energy you must exert is worth the potential benefit of crossing these interpersonal divides. Once you have decided that you want to lessen the interpersonal divide, undertake actions to make that happen. These may include participating in personal and optional professional and social activities with your colleagues, finding common areas of interest to discuss and be proactive about, and getting to know and be known by your colleagues. Remember, these and other such activities are all investments in your corporate future. Similarly, refraining from making any investment also comes with a cost.

Build trust. Learning to trust others may be one of the most difficult challenges for some African Americans. Throughout this book we have enumerated various reasons why trust may be tenuous between black professionals and many of their colleagues. However, there is no denying that trust is the cornerstone for building and maintaining relationships and cultivating professional interactions. Therefore African Americans have to find ways to move beyond issues of trust if they are to become more effective in the workplace. Failure to do so may render black leaders ineffective, mentally exhausted, and ultimately lonely. Without trusted colleagues to whom you can vent and with whom you can share advice and experiences, you are left to negotiate the corporate milieu alone.

Building trust is not easy. It entails giving up a modicum of control and this means making yourself vulnerable to others. For blacks this can be a frightening prospect. Who can afford to be deceived, let down, or otherwise negatively affected by others who may prove

---

Building Relationships

Find ways to bridge the gap.

Build trust.

Don't label other blacks.

Be bicultural.

---

untrustworthy? However, despite the need to protect yourself, you have to be realistic—you have to trust someone, and not just other blacks. To expand your sphere of trust, consider the following steps. Determine what information, tasks, or confidences you are willing to trust others with. Identify individuals who have proven themselves trustworthy. You might learn who these individuals are by reputation or by your own observations or experiences. If you are reluctant, begin trusting others with small things and gradually increase what you entrust to them as they continue to prove themselves. Also recognize that sometimes people just make mistakes. In these cases you might want to give others the benefit of the doubt or seriously consider the facts before assuming they have intentionally broken your trust. Perhaps the most important factors to consider are your own trustworthiness and your willingness to see others as trustworthy.

Don't label other blacks. One of the major issues that blacks face in corporate America is being labeled by others. Often they tend to blame whites or other non-blacks as the source of these stereotypes. However, blacks also engage in labeling one another and add to the dilemma by labeling non-blacks as well. Stereotypes, from whatever source, skew or obscure individuals' perceptions and expectations of others. Too often blacks label other African Americans when they feel they do not live up to expectations. For whatever reason, they may decide that their black colleagues are "too white" or "too black" or "too [fill in the blank]," coming up with any number of pejorative labels to describe them. Similarly, African Americans may unfairly characterize whites or other non-blacks, supposing that these others possess certain ideas or participate in specific, usually unflattering, behaviors.

The challenge and opportunity for black leaders is to set an example by recognizing, accepting, and promoting the rich diversity in every member of the organization. This starts with viewing people as individuals rather than as just representatives of a larger group. We are not suggesting that you ignore or devalue ethnic, cultural, gender, or other group associations. But we are advising that you first consider and value an individual's uniqueness, and not be disconcerted when that person's behaviors or ideas fall outside your expectations for representatives of their group.

Be bicultural. Learning how to move with apparent ease between different cultural groups and settings has been the key to success for many black leaders. This does not entail giving up your own culture or identity, but it does mean learning and adopting the behavioral norms of different cultures as you deem appropriate. For example, you might use black slang at home while avoiding it in business meetings unless you are using it to make a specific point. You might order calamari or a romaine salad with artichoke hearts at a business lunch; however, you wouldn't expect those items to show up on the menu at Big Mama's Soul Food Shack. Seriously, as we suggest in Chapter Seven, it is imperative for black leaders to understand the context in which they must work and to act appropriately. Being biculturally adept, then, also involves knowing when and where to employ your various cultural behaviors. This will enable you to more effectively negotiate different environments and situations and enhance your ability to communicate—providing an avenue for you to both speak and hear in the language of the moment.

9

What Colleagues Need to Know

The Negro problem! Of course, no one refers to it this way any more—at least not publicly. That does not mean, however, that people no longer see blacks as being problematic. As *Leading in Black and White* has outlined, many of the issues African Americans face in today's workplace are subtle. Consequently, people who are not black may not see them, and as a result, these people may choose to believe that difficulties don't exist. When racial difficulties do surface, these same people may decide to ignore them, assuming the problems are not theirs to solve. Thus the issue of black people—or "the problem"—casually shifts back to the shoulders of African Americans.

To blacks, others' inability to see race-related issues in the workplace is often perplexing, especially when whites and others have seemingly little difficulty identifying, understanding, and working through the subtle differences of many work-related social and political issues. Of course, these are unlikely to be issues in which they may be personally, if unknowingly, complicit or naively unaware. For example, recently a colleague of ours was describing the effects of living in another culture. He talked about the inconveniences and irritations of living and working abroad, which although relatively minor, together added up to culture shock. He urged his colleagues to recognize that culture shock is real and that it has real effects on people—influencing how they do their work and live their lives. People listening to him nodded their heads knowingly; this was something invisible that they could now see. Yet when issues of difference are charged with assertions of inequality, blacks and other nontraditional leaders may find their concerns are met with blank stares or surprise. Whether this perceived phenomenon comes as a result of white colleagues being less emotionally involved or perhaps liable, the result is that this inability (or unwillingness) to see and explore issues of workplace inequality often leaves black leaders feeling frustrated.

Just as African Americans have to deal with some uncomfortable questions and truths about their behaviors, responsibilities, and expectations in the workplace, other groups must also challenge themselves. Non-blacks have to ask themselves about their own responsibility in perpetuating attitudes, behaviors, and systems that benefit their own groups while quietly disempowering others. Non-blacks, and particularly whites, need to acknowledge their part in creating and maintaining the miasma within which many groups suffer. They also should recognize that "the problem" is not just "the Negro problem," but a shared problem that affects the entire organization. It is a problem that affects human resources, retention rates, creativity, and the organization's competitive stance. Ultimately, it affects the bottom line.

This chapter outlines strategies we believe can help dispel blindness to difference—the mind-set that contributes to miasma. These recommendations and strategies are organized in terms of self-development, education, and behavior, similar categories offered to black readers in Chapter Eight. We have purposely paralleled the structure of the previous chapter to reinforce the truth that *everyone* has work to do. Keep in mind, furthermore, that the following list is not exhaustive. It is intended to be a set of prompts to stimulate your thinking about what will be appropriate and effective in your particular context—your relationships, your department, and your organization.

Self-Development

We believe being comfortable with difference requires understanding oneself as well as those who are different. The following suggestions detail ways to explore your understanding of attitudes about difference and behaviors in response to it.

Understand that difference really does matter. It is important to recognize that when you are different, that difference really does matter, and it can affect virtually every aspect of your life. Helen Thompson, program manager for a national chemical company, sums up many blacks' experience when she says, "I don't think that there is a day that goes by that I'm not reminded that I'm black in this country." Another African American corporate manager recalls a similar insight she had when she first attended a black college. After her first month she noticed that because of the nearly all-black environment, she felt almost physically different, lighter somehow. "I finally realized that for the first time in my life, I wasn't dealing with race. I wasn't carrying it around with me, seeing it in others' eyes," she said. "It was wonderful, and I wondered if this is what it felt like to be white and not have to think of race every day, almost every moment." Being black, being different, is a pervasive experience. There is no getting away from it, and it has an effect on individuals internally—how they view and react to the world around them. However, there is more to it than just the internal components. Those who are different must be constantly aware of how others respond to them, and must consider this going into almost every situation. Recognizing that this reality exists for your black colleagues can be your first step toward creating a better relationship with them, as you not only understand the strain their difference can bring but also accept them for who they are.

Be willing to broaden your outlook. In a workplace that is becoming increasingly diverse and global, focusing solely on your own knowledge or experiences or those of a particular identity group (whether defined by race, economics, religion, gender, or some other factor) can be limiting. The prevailing concept that the United States, and therefore each of its workplaces, is a vast melting pot is inaccurate. This country is more like a tossed salad, each ingredient distinct but contributing to the whole. Says Tina Williams, a clinical psychologist, "There are more ways than the white way. . . . There are brown, black, blue, and green ways. Allow people to be themselves." A melting-pot mentality contributes to an assumption of similarity that ignores and devalues the reality of difference. When corporate citizens fail to recognize and appreciate the value of the difference that others bring with them into the work environment, they perpetuate the frustrations that black and other nontraditional executives experience as a result of having their uniqueness denied. And the valuable asset that this perspective of difference brings goes underutilized. In the new global economy, diversity is strength—a necessity.

Don't overassume similarities. Although it is important for groups to recognize their similarities, it is also important for them to honor and respect their differences. Making assumptions about similarities often means you may not truly be appreciating others or respecting individual differences. When people make unsubstantiated leaps to find commonalities, even their best intentions may go sadly awry. In your efforts to bridge the gulf of difference, you may, for example, assume a false similarity by adopting behaviors you believe are representative of a group. This might mean mimicking what you perceive to be another group's mannerisms as a way of "connecting" with them. In regard to your black colleagues, examples of this ill-conceived behavior are routinely greeting them or their family members by giving them "high fives" or using slang that is not part of your normal vocabulary. Such behaviors are annoying and almost always offensive.

On a related note, don't assume that because someone shares your gender, job title, or hometown that you and he are inherently

Self-Development
Understand that difference really does matter.
Be willing to broaden your outlook.
Don't overassume similarities.
Keep issues in perspective.
Don't expect blacks to fail.
Stretch your comfort zone.
Keep mutual respect paramount.

alike. As discussed in Chapter Four, unwarranted familiarity has adversely affected relationships between white women and women of color. Some white women believe they can speak for all women without regard for or in many cases understanding of the different experiences their sisters of color are having. Though it is true that many women's issues cut across racial, religious, and ethnic lines, to assume that the white female executive's reality is the only one that exists is to grossly underestimate and diminish the significance of the experience of executive women of color.

Keep issues in perspective. When talking to African Americans, it is important to appreciate the difference between individual concerns and matters of race. Be careful not to hold individual blacks responsible for national racial issues or assume that their personal perspective represents their group's—or that they even have an opinion on every racial issue. At some point almost every African American working in a corporate environment has been pinned to the wall by someone demanding an explanation for the behaviors of Jesse Jackson or Louis Farrakhan or the random blacks seen on the news or at the local mall. Closer to home, whites regularly call on blacks to explain the behaviors, attitudes, and work performance of other African Americans in the organization. They probably don't know these people, and even if they do, they are not responsible for others' behaviors or accountable to you. In a similar vein it is important to understand that when a black person champions an issue it is not necessarily a black issue. Be careful not to arbitrarily introduce race as an element in issues where it does not belong, or assume that race is an underlying theme in everything blacks discuss. Remember, what makes an issue racial is its content, not its messenger.

Don't expect blacks to fail. When it comes to race, it is critical to be honest with yourself about your assumptions and expectations. Don't assume that African Americans are underqualified, unwilling to excel, or going to fail. The truth is, some will fail and some will not, just like the members of any other racial, gender, or cultural group. Like others, African Americans will include some people who are sharp and some who are dull; there will be some who are prepared and some who are not. And when someone black does fail, that is never preordained by race. The failure could be due to any number of reasons. It may be a result of lack of that person's competency or preparation. In some cases the corporate context may have been construed to produce failure, or at the very least to stifle productivity. This person may have failed because everyone expected her to do so and consequently did not give her the support she needed. The point is that as a professional, you need to check your own beliefs and expectations about the success and failure of black colleagues to see if maybe, just maybe, the problem lies with you and not with them.

Stretch your comfort zone. Recognize that if a cross-race relationship is going to grow, you and not the other person may have to be the one to change. Be willing to meet African Americans on their own terms and not just your own. If you are the leader, this may mean being open to assigning blacks to roles or responsibilities for which they have not been previously considered. You might also explore and challenge stereotypes and other assumptions you have

about blacks and other nontraditional leaders. Then make a con-
certed effort, based on individual performance and contributions,
to evaluate your direct reports more equitably. If you are a peer or
the direct report of an African American executive, you need to be
willing to follow his lead, respecting both him and his decisions. In
either case give blacks and others who are different the same consideration you are willing to extend to white males—the predomi-
nant group of leaders in the organization.

Keep mutual respect paramount. Treat people as you would like
to be treated. This might seem a fairly simple rule, easy for all to follow and find value in. However, some blacks believe respect is hard
to come by. Consider that in our survey, over half the respondents
did not feel their identity as blacks was respected or appreciated
in their organizations. This point, coupled with the other evidence
we have presented throughout *Leading in Black and White*, speaks
volumes about the experiences of many of your black colleagues
every day.

   In seeking to contribute to a more equitable work environment
for blacks and other nontraditional leaders, or even just to enhance
relationships, you might, first, want to examine the degree and
manner in which you mete out respect to others. You can do this by
paying attention to how you communicate. Consider your language
and others' verbal and nonverbal responses, and ask for feedback as
appropriate. You might also show interest in others' lives, projects,
and aspirations rather than assuming they are only interested in
yours. Another way to show respect is to simply listen. Listen to
blacks' ideas as well as their concerns, and genuinely share your
opinions.

   Respect is one of those fundamental benefits individuals automatically expect to be granted—although it can then be lost. Sometimes, particularly when there is rampant distrust, small cultural
mannerisms can have significant meanings. Small things, such as
whether you put your change on the counter or put it in the sales-
clerk's hand, suggest your level of respect. Whether you regularly talk

directly with your black colleagues or tend to use intermediaries may reflect the degree of respect you have for them. Respect is not synonymous with liking someone. You are not expected to like every black person you meet, nor can you expect each one to like you; but each of you should be confident of receiving a certain level of respect that enables you to be productive and collaborative members of your organization.

Education

People often assume that because they work with other groups they also understand them. Unfortunately that assumption is erroneous more often than not. To understand other groups, you should educate yourself about them and you have to be willing to learn, even when the new information seems to be at odds with what you already know. To be truly educated you must also be willing to learn more about yourself than you may be comfortable with. The following are suggestions about ways to learn about African Americans and hints about some of the things you may wish or need to know about yourself. Learning about groups and the individuals within that group are two different things. For professionals in an increasingly diverse workplace, both pursuits are important: the former to help you develop closer relationships with African American colleagues, the latter to help you develop a more inclusive perspective of the changing dynamics of the workforce in general.

Learn about blacks and miasma. Read about, listen to, attend events with, and generally just get to know African Americans. Come at this discovery unbegrudgingly, with an open mind, and with your assumptions checked at the door. Take an inquiry approach that suggests that you are asking questions and gathering information with a willingness to learn. This does not necessarily mean that you should pepper your black colleagues with incessant questions. As you build close relationships with African Americans, you may find yourself getting into discussions about race. As you

Education
Learn about blacks and miasma.
Question your own perspectives.
Seek feedback about your behaviors.
Be aware of your context.

engage in these conversations, be aware of your assumptions so they don't impede your learning and communication processes. Joanna Gayle, vice president at a national financial institution, says she wants people to *know* her, not just what is on paper about her. Wilson Davis, lead technical specialist for a major tobacco company, adds that he wants people to understand his experience more completely: "They don't really know what it's like to be black, to grow up as a colored person, grow up to become Negro, and then evolve to be black. If they understood that better, we would have more harmony at work." In truth, learning, in-depth exploratory examination, is imperative if people are going to work more effectively with each other. But this learning is not likely to happen unless all parties involved trust each other enough to share. That comes with time and honest outreach.

Question your own perspectives. Check your own perspectives about race and roles. What are the assumptions behind your thoughts and behaviors? Do you assume, for instance, that because someone is African American she has an intimate knowledge of the cultures and customs of African nations? When you promote nontraditional leaders, do you bask in the pride of *your* accomplishment, as if you have done them a favor? Finally, do you habitually relegate African Americans and other nontraditional leaders to "acting" or "assistant" positions of authority rather than granting them the full responsibility and authority that you regularly bestow upon white males? Before you answer this last question, you should know that CCL research suggests that white males are indeed less likely than African Americans and white women to be given an acting or assistant role initially. Often people are unaware of the deeply ingrained beliefs that subtly guide their behaviors. Almost without conscious thought, these beliefs shape their decisions about who is fit for certain responsibilities. Most whites do not intentionally think "this person is an African American so she's not ready for this job." They just simply do not give her the job. That behavior, whether they intend it to be or not, whether it is conscious or not, is racism.

Seek feedback about your behaviors. Find trusted agents—nontraditionals among them—who can help you understand how your cross-racial, cross-gender, or cross-anything interactions are perceived (see Chapter Four). Ask them to give you feedback on how you come across in general or how you handled a particular situation. You can also use your trusted agents as sounding boards to help you determine the best course of action prior to dealing with particular issues or situations. Of course you need to have a relationship with this black person before you approach him for feedback. Remember that your trusted agents can speak only from their individual points of view. No one African American is the voice of black America. Each person, though, may be able to give you insights into how some African Americans might feel about your issue and why. However, be sensitive about whether you have established enough trust and intimacy with your trusted agents to have these conversations without putting them on the hot seat.

Be aware of your context. Familiarize yourself with the written and unwritten rules of your organization and consider what they mean for your African American colleagues. Who has access? Who has visibility? Who organizes formal and informal events? Who guides the corporate culture? By becoming better aware and understanding the context in which you and your black and other colleagues must work, you can gain insight into and appreciation for their perspectives and reactions. As you pay more attention to your context, also take pains to become aware of events that are happening beyond your specific area of responsibility.

Behavior

Self-awareness, education, and behavior are certainly important when we are discussing cross-race relations. Perhaps most important are the relationships between and among people. What can you do to create, enhance, or maintain a relationship? Much of the advice we offer suggests simple things such as respecting people, not being motivated by fear, and having a willingness to change yourself. It is from these positive intentions that behavioral changes in attitudes, communications, and interactions will develop. Combined, they can stimulate a more inclusive and effective work environment for all people.

Communicate openly and provide feedback. Remember that communication is best when it is two-way. So, listen to and seriously consider all perspectives, and share your insights with black managers in a way that is engaging, not condescending. Communicate openly with your African American colleagues. Be as honest with them as you are with other colleagues, and provide fair and objective feedback. If praise and encouragement are due, don't be stingy. If developmental feedback is called for, back it up with data and don't worry about accusations of racism. If you are being accused of racist behavior because of the feedback you are giving to another, you might, first, check your motivation for giving this person feedback, and assess the manner in which you do so. Would you, honestly, give the same feedback if the person looked more like you? Would you give it in the same way? If the answer to these questions is yes, you might then ask yourself if you have the data to support this feedback about the person's behavior and the impact it is having on the workplace. Finally, consider whether you are willing to help this person improve on the issues the feedback addresses. If you can comfortably answer yes to all these questions, you should give the person appropriate feedback, regardless of his or her protests of racism.

Don't limit interactions with black colleagues. We suggest you get to know your black colleagues better. You might start by going to their offices and chatting for a while about general business and perhaps even casual or personal matters, at a level where you both feel comfortable. As your interactions become more frequent and, we hope, increasingly unguarded, you might find that the subjects become more sensitive or personal. In this case continue to be open and to share. Listen to what these other people have to say about these various subjects without rushing to judgment, being defensive, or alienating them. Reflect your intent to foster a broader relationship and understanding with them, not just through your words but also through your actions.

As we discussed in Chapter Six, African Americans have fewer opportunities to mentor or be mentored by others. Therefore another way of expanding your interactions with blacks is to take the leap, if you haven't done so already, and mentor someone you feel has promise. At the same time, be willing to be mentored by an African American leader. Black leaders can provide you with insights and skill development just as their more traditional counterparts can. By increasing your interactions with blacks and by making these interactions both formal and informal, you have a greater chance of enhancing your work effectiveness simply because you have a better knowledge of each other's styles and skill levels.

Allow for differences. Strive to accept African Americans in their entirety, without filtering their blackness or presupposing behaviors and setting expectations. This means that saying to someone, or even believing, "I don't see you as black; I just see you as a regular person" is not a compliment. Being black is not a characteristic that needs to be overlooked as if it were an unsightly blemish or a scar to diplo-

Behavior
Communicate openly and provide feedback.
Don't limit interactions with black colleagues.
Allow for differences.
Don't be afraid.
Recognize and support "average" African Americans.
Demand and enforce equitable treatment.
Be a change agent.

matically ignore. Blackness is an integral part of a person's being. It helps to shape the person's perspectives and typically helps define who the person is. Although blackness is not all an African American is, it is certainly a significant aspect and quality for that person. In the quest for a more inclusive and equitable organization, however, many leaders have gone too far in equating equality with sameness. Also contributing to this assumption of similarity may be people's discomfort with issues of difference in general and race in particular.

In a 1999 HR *Magazine* article, "If Diversity, Then Higher Profits?" Sherry Kuczynski explains that governmental regulatory policies and organizations focus on diversity initiatives that "strive to be color blind and gender blind and encourage people to see each other as 'just the same as everyone else.'" The problem, she says, "is that everyone is not the same." This reality of difference has got to be acknowledged. And more than that, the differences need to be appreciated and valued for their benefit to the organization. As Henry Wate, a manager of a major chemical company, says, "Be receptive to other insights and perspectives . . . because people are very talented and what we need to do is trust that their talent will bring you the kinds of contributions and impact that you're looking for."

Don't be afraid. Don't allow unfounded fear or discomfort to control your actions. When these emotions guide you, your well-intentioned behaviors can be viewed as awkward and may be subject to unflattering misinterpretations. For example, don't refrain from speaking to a black friend because she is with a group of other African Americans. Likewise, don't feel compelled to make a meaningless comment to blacks sitting together at a lunch table, because of your unease in seeing them together. Instead be aware of when you are feeling uncomfortable, try to uncover the source of the discomfort, and try to manage it. Determine whether there is a logical basis for your concerns. If not, develop a plan to get beyond these emotions. Ask others to help you implement your plan. Build yourself a support network comprising nontraditional leaders and others who can encourage and advise you. A good place to start is with your trusted agents. If you aren't quite comfortable making initial overtures to colleagues, you might find it easier looking outside the organization for support. Regardless, be open with your fears and even with your desires (if applicable) to overcome them. Exploring new territory with someone you trust and with whom you can be open can be a great source of strength and encouragement.

Recognize and support "average" African Americans. Although some African American professionals achieve superstar status in organizations, it should come as no surprise that the majority of their black colleagues, like the majority of their white colleagues, are average, well-intentioned contributors to the company. Many of these "average" blacks believe they are being overlooked due to their race, because they see whites who are not extraordinarily talented move ahead faster and farther than they do. Although it may be true that the black superstars find both organizational opportunity and support to showcase their talents, not all black managers find the workplace as open, supportive, and accessible for upward mobility or recognition—not even to the extent of their *average* white colleagues. Nan Blunt, a manager for an executive development firm, told us that what gives her anxiety in the workplace is her concern about blacks who are just starting out or who are hard, average workers. "What happens if you just happen to be a black person who is just as good as other white people?" asked Blunt. If her concerns are well founded, it could mean that there is a storehouse of African Americans, and other nontraditional leaders, whose contributions may be undervalued and who themselves may be ignored, to the detriment of the organization's overall effectiveness.

To ensure that every member of the organization has an opportunity to excel, you may need to rethink some assumptions and review some of your behaviors. Examine the criteria you use for selecting those you will nurture or develop for the next level of responsibility. Consider how much time and energy you spend on those you consider average—are they being overlooked? Provide the same opportunities for all the average members of your organization, and support their efforts, regardless of their differences. For in doing so you enhance your organization's productivity by fully engaging its most valuable resource.

Demand and enforce equitable treatment.   As a professional concerned with issues of diversity, support individuals or coalitions that are seeking equitable treatment. Every member of the organization has the right to be treated equitably. If you or others believe this is not happening, check your perceptions and document (when you can) the difference in treatment. If you are not a decision maker or policy enforcer, refer the matter to the appropriate individual or department in your company. If after seeking help you do not believe the issue is being adequately addressed, go outside to an external agency for help or guidance.

If you are in a position to do so as a leader, set policies that foster equitable corporate practices. In your own realm, encourage and enforce equitable practice in hiring, promotions, visibility, and job tasks and assignments.

Be a change agent.   If you are a leader, especially if you are a traditional leader, use your status to become a change agent. Change is less threatening when it comes from within—changes in policy appear less radical when they come from a member of the mainstream. To be an effective change agent, you need to have established strong credibility. Remember, trust and accomplishments are requisites for garnering credibility, but don't be surprised if, as you work to produce change, your accomplishments increase and you receive greater trust from a more diverse group of colleagues. Being recognized as a visionary can strengthen your leadership role and influence.

10

What Organizations Need to Know

That people are involved in issues of race is intuitively obvious. That organizations are also involved is obvious to some but not to all. An organization plays an influential role in the mind-set of its workforce. It puts systems into place, creates and enforces policies, and fashions a general atmosphere that quickly lets people know what behaviors and attitudes are permissible and rewarded. However, that inequity exists in many organizations is a fact that often goes unnoticed and undiscussed. According to "Race in the Workplace," an article by Robert J. Grossman, "racial tensions are often unacknowledged but lurk in the shadows around issues that [HR managers are] asked to investigate and mediate." Grossman goes on to quote an HR professional who suggests organizations are more interested in "looking good rather than doing good" with their diversity initiatives, and are less concerned with identifying "root causes" than they are with simply avoiding trouble. In sum, organizations may not be fully aware of or willing to acknowledge or address the issues of difference, nor do they deal with the associated difficulties that this, sometimes benign, neglect creates.

Beyond setting policies to establish and support equity in the workplace, organizations—embodied through the actions and decisions of their senior executives—set the climate for maintaining and enforcing these policies. If an organization is to make strides in working across the racial divide, then its senior executives must be willing to stretch, and perhaps be uncomfortable, as they strive to gain new perspectives that will illuminate the invisible issues affecting their black and other nontraditional employees. By being willing to be uncomfortable, we mean that these executives must be prepared to take a hard look at themselves and the practices of their organization from a point of view that is not steeped in the traditions and understandings of predominantly white male privilege. It is not an easy task to move outside your personal and cultural understanding. Yet increasingly, as the country browns and becomes more diverse, it is a critical task.

This chapter looks at some of the strategies and guidelines that senior executives and human resource departments should consider as they strive to make their workplaces more than just legally compliant. These suggestions are intended to prompt executives' thinking toward ideas and actions that can guide their corporations in developing a more fully inclusive, open atmosphere.

As in the earlier chapters we suggest strategies that focus on education and behavior. However, because this chapter deals with organizational rather than personal dynamics, we have not included a section on developing relationships. The following sections on education and behavior are designed to provide organizations with a strategic view of how miasma in the workplace is experienced by blacks and other nontraditional leaders. They also examine how the demands of the environment may affect these *different* leaders. Furthermore, these sections explore how the most senior members of the company can cultivate an environment that diffuses the murky atmosphere that clouds effective and equitable treatment of employees and their issues.

Education

This section outlines educational strategies for senior executives and human resource departments to aid them in their capacity as policymakers and enforcers in the organization. At their core these

Education
Understand that isolation causes stress.
Understand that diversity is more than propaganda.
Acknowledge and respect the power of miasma.
Recognize the impact of the Good Ole Boy Network.
Don't expect too much from formal mentoring programs.

strategies describe efforts that inform the system through its senior people.

Understand that isolation causes stress. To make any meaningful strides toward creating an equitable workplace, organizations must first recognize that there is extra pressure on African Americans who work in settings where they are isolated from other blacks. This may be as true for senior executives who are black as it is for people who serve in lower-level capacities. Being alone or one of few African Americans in the workplace often means being in the spotlight, knowing that one's successes and failures are highly visible. Isolation also means that there are few people with whom you can practice your own culture and with whom you can check your racial understandings. This is not to suggest that people, and blacks in particular, cannot develop strong cross-race relationships; rather it means that cross-race relationships are inherently different from same-race relationships, bringing with them different strengths and vulnerabilities. When an African American works with very few blacks, he is more likely to be aware of his difference and as a result more cognizant of the cost of any missteps that he might make. That awareness itself is costly, imposing more stress more of the time. The price for blacks, in many cases, is realized in reduced trust between colleagues; perceptions that they have to work twice as hard as their white counterparts; and the belief that they must often keep their guard up to protect themselves.

Understand that diversity is more than propaganda. People who run organizations need to view diversity as something integral to the survival of their organization in this millennium and not just propaganda. For those executives who see diversity as a trend, part of a politically correct movement they believe will disappear in a few years, diversity initiatives will likely not bear much fruit. To see and use diversity mainly as propaganda is to display a deep misunderstanding and misevaluation of the reasons why people are pushing for more workplace inclusion. Additionally, seeing and using diversity in this way has the potential to create great cynicism among African Americans and other nontraditional leaders in the workforce when they see that the organization does not mean what it says. In an age when the battle for retention is being constantly waged, anything that gives employees impetus to leave your organization is dangerous. Beyond retention, there are political and legal benefits for fair practices. For many industries there are also marketplace and client benefits. From our point of view as authors and researchers in the leadership field, the most important reason is that fair and inclusive workplaces free people from concerns about lack of equity so that they can focus all their energies and talents on the work at hand.

Acknowledge and respect the power of miasma. Much of what happens with African Americans is not clearly visible to those with more traditional experiences. Organizations that wish to be inclusive must learn to value African American and other perspectives, even when the senior executives themselves cannot clearly see the issues to which the nontraditional employees are alluding. At some point organizations need to learn to honor the fact that African Americans and others can interpret their own experiences. Often when blacks interpret an incident one way and someone else views it differently, the African American is told she is being too sensitive or that the event did not occur the way she saw it. Rarely do people say, "Well, I didn't see it that way, but perhaps we should investigate more fully." If executives learn to see and respect what is "fuzzy," what is miasmic, they may be less likely to automatically assume that their position is correct and they may be more willing to notice alternate perspectives. By acknowledging that African Americans and others may have a valid viewpoint, organizations are likely to engender greater respect, efficiency, loyalty, individual achievement, and group creativity. Additionally, the very exercise of exploring alternative perspectives can help the organization to become more innovative in that it can push people beyond their conventional way of thinking.

Recognize the impact of the Good Ole Boy Network. This unofficial network is recognized as a reality and discussed by many people at all levels of the corporate ladder. Organizations need to recognize that despite whatever good the network may do the organization, its by-product is exclusion. That exclusion often results in limited vision, limited perspective, nepotism, failure to retain employees, and division within the ranks. Senior executives—and indeed all managers—need to educate themselves about exactly who gets into and who is left out of this network. Everyone should have the same opportunity to gain access to your organization's inner circle. If some people lack equal opportunity, your organization is, at best, underutilizing talented professionals and, at worst, creating circumstances under which people are willing to leave to go to organizations that do offer equal opportunities.

Don't expect too much from formal mentoring programs. Many organizations have instituted formal mentoring programs with the hope of benefiting all employees. As discussed in Chapter Six, these programs are often initiated because the organization recognizes that African Americans and others are not being mentored through informal channels. Although the idea behind these programs is good, it is important to realize that formal mentoring will not be a panacea for all race-related problems or other issues of difference. It is true that mentoring programs can open doors for people who might not have had such opportunities. However, much of the effectiveness of mentoring depends on the chemistry between the two individuals involved, and chemistry can't be legislated. Further, even if the program is a success, mentoring by itself cannot take the place of strong and fair policies, attitudes, and behaviors throughout the company.

Behavior

Organizational behaviors are key to creating an atmosphere in which all employees can thrive. The following strategies suggest that policies of inclusion, of honoring difference, and of regularly gathering organizational feedback can help companies create a more open work environment.

Challenge inclusion issues.   Senior executives set the tone for the organization. This being so, they need to articulate and enforce the goal of inclusion both in their inner circle and in the organization at large. It is up to senior executives to create opportunities for access to the inner circle. It is also up to this group to ensure that all employees are considered to be mentoring prospects. Senior executives need to determine whether they are willing to push aggressively for people of difference. They also have to decide how they will handle any pushback from the traditionally advantaged population. Make sure people who are pushing back are thoroughly heard. Be willing to listen to their concerns. However, if their concerns are based largely on fear or privilege, reiterate and stand by the company policy. If their concerns are valid, address them. When the organization makes a commitment to an inclusive strategy, it has to be willing to stick with it even when many in the company are not pleased with the decision. In essence, senior executives and HR practitioners who are not black will benefit from reading and practicing the strategies outlined in Chapter Nine and in the sections titled "What Colleagues Can Do" in Chapters Two through Seven.

Behavior
Challenge inclusion issues.
Develop and periodically check organizational policies.
Honor and promote difference.
Link diversity management to consequences.
Take top-down as well as bottom-up approaches.
Link inclusiveness to business strategy.

Develop and periodically check organizational policies. Although policy cannot legislate attitudes, it can influence behavior. When developing policies that address the need and desire for equity in the organization, make sure the diverse groups have input into the drafting and reviewing of diversity initiatives. Solicit their input when preparing policies for fair hiring practices, appraisal processes, and other areas where groups typically relegated to silence have much that is insightful to say. Furthermore, ensure that the organization has adequate means for people to report and seek redress for racial and other issues. To honestly foster a welcoming approach to diversity, organizations need to set policy in the light of what they want to happen—not out of fear of what they want to avoid.

Just as people typically improve when they get believable feedback about their behaviors, so do organizations. Organizations must maintain equal standards and opportunities for all. But the hardest work may come with monitoring and enforcing equity issues. Organizations and executives concerned with true workplace equity need to actively monitor the work environment, including hiring, compensation, and promotion practices, and be willing to take necessary steps to correct infractions or acknowledge or reward adherence. Conduct culture surveys that include questions about difference and other issues of import to the organization. Tools you might consider include the Campbell™ Organizational Survey, the Denison Organizational Culture Survey, and CCL's own KEYS® to Creativity. Request that the data be sorted by race and other salient characteristics such as gender. Sometimes, even on questions that are not race centered, companies find that racial or other groups perceive the organization's culture differently from the general population. Use the data from the survey to help you create, review, or understand the impact of policies currently in effect. Don't allow people to undermine blacks or other nontraditional leaders by circumventing them, disrespecting them, or by ignoring their decisions.

Honor and promote difference. There are many formal and informal ways to respect difference in an organization. Companies can encourage affinity networks for African Americans and others; these groups can champion changes for their members, encourage networking and professional growth, and function as cultural safe houses. Honor difference by educating the members of your organization about differences. Such education should go beyond simple statements of acknowledgment and extend to understanding, valuing, and inviting these differences. Find ways to facilitate learning about all cultures and perspectives represented, including those that are dominant in the organization. To find out more about the diverse cultures represented by the people who make up your company, read, research, and talk with these people. Then acknowledge and celebrate holidays equally, being sure to respectfully consider the nuances that each of the different perspectives brings. Note different traditions and perspectives that groups have. Find ways for these viewpoints to be reflected or respected in the business or culture of the organization. Disseminate this information through intranet sites, all-staff meetings, office e-mails, and bulletin boards, and allow people to share their own uniqueness in their own way as appropriate. In essence, find ways to enrich your organization by creating, promoting, or enforcing policies that educate your workforce and ensure that every employee has an equal opportunity to fully contribute.

Link diversity management to consequences. Often diversity and equity issues are not identified as goals for managers. To encourage the adoption of tolerance and the repetition of fair and equitable behavior, take an active stance toward diversity issues. Link both positive and negative actions to consequences to encourage a culture of growth. Take even-handed, punitive action against discriminatory practices. Doing so can check discriminatory actions before they have the opportunity to spread and infect corporate morale. Limited consequences (slaps on the wrist) following discriminatory acts are unlikely to motivate behavioral change. At the same time, acknowledging and rewarding effective initiatives that take equity and diversity issues into consideration can promote and reinforce desirable behavior. If successful diversity management fails to be acknowledged, there will be little or no incentive for its repetition or for others to adopt the practices throughout the organization.

Take top-down as well as bottom-up approaches. To ensure a fully equitable workplace and to foster the awareness of miasma, diversity management needs to occur at all levels of an organization. It should become shared knowledge, a skill developed in and required of all managers. Corporate culture may be inspired from the top down, but it is implemented and kept alive in the day-to-day workings of the middle and lower echelons. As Mary-Frances Winters, president of The Winters Group, explains in her article "Sustaining Inclusion," many diversity plans call for training, recruitment, and promotion strategies to increase the ranks of underutilized groups and leadership development to help managers understand how to lead diverse employees effectively. Although such efforts are necessary, they are insufficient. The top-down approach can lead to resistance. Line managers often cannot see how to implement global strategies. Employees return to their work teams from diversity training with heightened awareness but unsure of what to do differently. The work team itself, however, can provide the best environment in which to apply concepts and generate real learning. Creating opportunities for work groups to explore and act on diversity issues as they relate to the work team gives people the opportunity to practice and reinforce their learnings. Giving people this ability to customize their efforts enhances their chances of achieving goals of equity and inclusiveness.

Link inclusiveness to business strategy. In his book *Creating the Multicultural Organization*, Taylor Cox identifies at least five areas in which diversity positively affects organizations. Although it is true that organizations that acknowledge diversity may experience increased difficulties in communication and conflict because of differences, Cox asserts that the potential benefits far outweigh any costs. In sum, he argues the benefits are realized through improved problem solving and decision making, greater creativity and innovation, increased organizational flexibility, better use of human talent, and enhanced marketing strategies.

What should be clear, both from Cox's research and from the information we have sought to share throughout *Leading in Black and White*, is that the true value in inclusiveness is not about political correctness; it is about giving credence to and respecting the differences of others while reaping significant organizational and personal benefits. Nontraditional leaders want to be accepted and fully used in the organization. When we asked black executives what they wanted their organizations to know most about them, their routine response could be summed up as, "I wish our organizations would recognize that we have the same core goals, values, and aspirations as they have." The majority of our interviewees shared two other salient points. First, they wanted the organization to succeed. And second, they wanted the people in the organization to see [blacks] as fellow human beings.

The challenge for corporate America therefore may be twofold: to acknowledge and respect the differences represented in the workplace, and to understand and value the benefits this diversity brings. Writes Clifton Taulbert, author of *Eight Habits of the Heart*, in an article for *Executive Excellence* magazine, "The changing demographics of our workplace and marketplace are also changing the ways we do business. To compete successfully, we must recognize and accommodate these changes, starting with the changing look of our customer base, acquisitions, and our strategic alliances. As a result of how we do business and the demands of these changes, we no longer have the 'luxury' of underutilizing employees. We need to harness the expertise of each person and see diversity as an asset." Further, he challenges the organization to think beyond its business motives to those that address individual responsibility as being at the core of creating and advocating change. Says Taulbert, "The business case for valuing our diversity will be validated by the bottom-line results, but will be sustained by our individual unselfish actions."

Appendix

Assessing Your Political Savvy

This Appendix contains an assessment tool reflecting the information in Chapter Seven, "Understanding the Political Landscape." This informal tool has been used in workshops conducted by the Center for Creative Leadership to enhance understanding and build awareness. It is offered here as an aid to understanding and using the information in Chapter Seven.

MANEUVERING THROUGH CORPORATE AMERICA

Politically savvy leaders must be aware of and understand the context and culture in which they are challenged to lead. They must also be aware of their own strengths and developmental needs, and they must be technically and interpersonally competent. The following strategies can assist leaders in their pursuit of greater insight into themselves and the environments in which they lead.

---

1. Understanding Your Environment: How well do you read your workplace?

Make a list of three or four significant issues (or issues you think may be of major importance in the near future) facing your organization. Then, without divulging your list, ask a trusted colleague whom you believe to be politically savvy to make a similar list. (A sample form for the colleague's list is provided at the end of this Appendix.) Get together with your colleague and compare and contrast your list and your colleague's list and discuss the differences and similarities. Revisit your list in one to two months to see how the issues on the lists have played out and then discuss them again with your trusted agent.

Your List

_____

_____

_____

_____

2. Understanding Yourself: Are you aware of yourself and how others experience you?

The keys to any effective self-analysis are honest feedback and self-disclosure. You may have tools at your disposal (within the organization) that can provide you with significant feedback about your individual preferences, style of leadership, ability to work with others and the desirability of your working with others, and personal motivation. You can use similar tools to gain a clearer picture of how others view you. Pay close attention to your appraisal—ask for specific examples or feedback about areas listed as strengths and areas requiring further development. Finally, attempt to be honest about what you *want* and what you *receive* from your current job. Work to decrease the gap between the two by taking responsibility for your *professional* and *personal* well-being.

3. Understanding Your Abilities: Are you competent in your role?

Use the scales that follow (or develop your own items) to rate yourself on the competencies listed and then ask one or more trusted colleagues to rate you on the same scales. (A sample form for your colleagues' ratings is provided at the end of this Appendix.) Then discuss with your colleagues both the areas in which their views are similar to yours and the areas in which their views differ. Remember, honesty is essential!

Rate each item on a 5-point scale where 1 is least satisfactory and 5 is most satisfactory.

Your Ratings

1. Accuracy/completeness of work	1	2	3	4	5
2. Timeliness of work	1	2	3	4	5
3. Knowledge to do the job	1	2	3	4	5
4. Ability to multitask	1	2	3	4	5
5. Gets the job done	1	2	3	4	5
6. Dependable and reliable	1	2	3	4	5

Continuously seek to balance the application of your interpersonal needs with the demands of the situation and the environment.

From: _____

Date: _____

To: _____

Dear Colleague:

Please make a list of three or four significant issues (or those you think may be of major importance in the near future) facing our organization. I am making a similar list and would like to compare my list with yours to discuss the similarities and differences.

Please List Your Responses Here

_____

_____

_____

_____

From: _____

Date: _____

To: _____

Dear Colleague:

I am seeking honest, informal feedback from you as a trusted friend about my current job performance. After I get your response, I would like to talk about specific ways in which I can improve my efforts or continue to model positive behavior.

Rate each item on a 5-point scale where 1 is least satisfactory and 5 is most satisfactory.

Your Ratings

1. Accuracy/completeness of work	1	2	3	4	5
2. Timeliness of work	1	2	3	4	5
3. Knowledge to do the job	1	2	3	4	5
4. Ability to multitask	1	2	3	4	5
5. Gets the job done	1	2	3	4	5
6. Dependable and reliable	1	2	3	4	5

References and Suggested Readings

America, R. F., & Anderson, B. E. (1996). *Soul in management: How African-American managers thrive in the competitive corporate environment*. Secaucus, NJ: Citadel Press, p. 8 quoted.

Bell, E.J.E., & Nkomo, S. M. (2001). *Our separate ways: Black and white women and the struggle for professional identity*. Boston: Harvard Business School Publishing, p. 13 quoted.

Branch, S. (1998, July 6). What blacks think of America. *Fortune*, pp. 140–143.

Campbell, D. (1974). *If you don't know where you're going, you'll probably end up somewhere else*. Allen, TX: Thomas More.

Catalyst. (1997). *Women of color in corporate management: A statistical picture*. New York: Author.

Cose, E. (2002). *The envy of the world: On being a black man in America*. New York: Washington Square Press.

Cox, T., Jr. (2001). *Creating the multicultural organization*. San Francisco: Jossey-Bass.

Douglas, C. (in press). *Lessons of a diverse workforce: A report on research and findings*. Greensboro, NC: Center for Creative Leadership.

Edwards, A., & Polite, C. K. (1992). *Children of the dream: The psychology of black success*. New York: Anchor Books, pp. 265 and 266 quoted.

Feagin, J. R., & Sikes, M. P. (1994). *Living with racism: The black middle class experience*. Boston: Beacon Press, p. 53 quoted.

Federal Glass Ceiling Commission. (1995, March). *Good for business: Making full use of the nation's human capital.* Washington, DC: U.S. Department of Labor.

Fernandez, J. P. (with Davis, J.). (1999). *Race, gender and rhetoric: The true state of race and gender relations in corporate America.* New York: McGraw-Hill, p. 243 quoted.

Grossman, R. J. (2000, March). Race in the workplace. *HR Magazine,* pp. 44–45.

Hammonds, K. (2000, December). Family values. *Fast Company,* pp. 168–182.

Hill, L. (1995, March). *Power dynamics in organizations* (Harvard Business School Case Note). Boston: Harvard Business School Publishing.

Kochman, T. (1981). *Black and white styles in conflict.* Chicago: University of Chicago Press.

Kuczynski, S. (1999, December). If diversity, then higher profits? *HR Magazine,* pp. 66–76.

Livers, A., & Brutus, S. (2000, March–April). Informal networking and the African American manager. *Leadership in Action,* pp. 1–30.

McCall, M. W., Lombardo, M. M., & Morrison, A. M. (1988). *The lessons of experience: How successful executives develop on the job.* Lexington, MA: Lexington Books.

Morrison, A. M. (1992). *The new leaders: Guidelines on leadership diversity in America.* San Francisco: Jossey-Bass.

Napolitano, C., & Henderson, L. (1998). *The leadership odyssey: A self-development guide to new skills for new times.* San Francisco: Jossey-Bass.

Parker, P. S., & Ogilvie, D. T. (1996). Gender, culture, and leadership: Toward a culturally distinct model of African-American women executives' leadership strategies. *Leadership Quarterly, 7*(2), pp. 189–214.

Richard, O. C., & Grimes, D. (1996, December). Bicultural interrole conflict: An organizational perspective. *Mid-Atlantic Journal of Business, 32*(3), pp. 155–171.

Senge, P., Kleiner, A., Roberts, C., Ross, R., & Smith, B. (1994). *The fifth discipline fieldbook.* New York: Doubleday/Currency.

Sue, D. W., & Sue, D. (1990). *Counseling the culturally different: Theory and practice* (2nd ed.). New York: Wiley.

Tatum, B. (1997). *"Why are all the black kids sitting together in the cafeteria?":* *A psychologist explains the development of racial identity.* New York: Basic Books, pp. 21 and 26 quoted.

Taulbert, C. (2002, March). Positive results. *Executive Excellence,* p. 140.

Thomas, D. A. (2001, April). The truth about mentoring minorities: Race matters. *Harvard Business Review,* pp. 99–107.

Thomas, D. A., & Gabarro, J. J. (1999). *Breaking through: The making of minority executives in corporate America.* Boston: Harvard Business School Publishing.

U.S. Census Bureau. (March 2000). Current population survey. Racial statistics population division. Table 11.

U.S. Department of Commerce. (September 1993). *We the Americans: Blacks.* Economics and statistics administration, Bureau of the Census, page 9.

Williams, L. (2000). *It's the little things: The everyday interactions that get under the skin of blacks and whites.* New York: Harcourt, p. 132 quoted.

Winters, M.-F. (2002, March). Sustaining inclusion. *Executive Excellence,* *19*(3), p. 11.

Index

86–89; suggestions for white colleagues on, 90–92; trust and, 87

"Race in the Workplace" (Grossman), 209

Racial issues, keeping in perspective, 196–197

Racial responsibility. *See* Responsibility-taking for other blacks

Racism: existence of, 178–179, 186; naivety about, 178–179; preoccupation with, 186–187; purposeful, 150; responding to accusations of, 203–204; subtle or unintentional, 149–150, 160–161, 179, 193–194, 201–202. *See also* Assumptions; Misperceptions; Stereotypes

"Raleigh, D.," 25, 86

"Ramsey, R.," 117

Recognition, of diversity management efforts, 216–217

Reinventing America, 36–37

Relationships: cross-race, 189–208, 211; expanding interactions and, 204; interpersonal distance in, 189–190; mentoring and, 116–136; networking and, 93–115; political savvy and, 137–164; race-gender issues and, 79–81, 84–86, 86–92; recognizing, as two-way street, 90; strategies and guidelines for black leaders and, 169–192; strategies and guidelines for white colleagues and, 193–208; tendency of people to form, with similar people, 99–100. *See also* Mentoring; Networking

Remembering, the people with whom you neBlack women:work, 112

Representative, racial, 68

Resilience, 188

Resistance, top-down approaches and, 217

Respect: giving equal, 72–73; organizational, 218–219; race-gender issues and, 80, 82, 90–91; by white colleagues, 199–200

Responsibility-taking for other blacks, 6, 47, 48–73; assumptions about, examining one's, 68–69, 71–72; awareness of others' expectations for, 69; belief that one can't make mistakes and, 23–25, 49; belief that one must work twice as hard and, 22–23, 51–55; black community expectations and, 64–63; community responsibilities and, 61–63; defensive mode and, 23–24; elements of, 50–63; experience of, unique to black leaders, 63–65; family responsibilities and, 60–61; leadership responsibilities and, 57–59; networking and, 57–58, 66–68, 95; organizational expectations for, 54–55, 123–124; organizational responsibilities and, 50–59; organizational tactics for dealing with, 66–70; overcompensation *versus*, 67–68; percentage of black leaders who feel, 49, 64, 65; personal development strategies for dealing with, 66–70; personal responsibilities and, 59–63, 69; politics and, 154–155; self-responsibility and, 59–60; stress of, 49–50, 54, 58–59, 64–65; suggestions for black leaders on, 66–70; suggestions for white colleagues on, 70–73; task responsibilities and, 51–55; team responsibilities and, 55–57; value of giving back and, 62–63, 69–70

Retention, honoring black identity and, 37, 212

Rewards: linking diversity management to, 216–217; racial responsibility and ensuring equal, 66–67, 70

Rice, C., 65

Risk: negotiating, 142–143; taking measured, 158

"Rogers, D.," 111, 141–142, 143, 146

Role models, black mentors as, 125–126

S

Safety, networking for, 103–104

Salary disparities, 83–84, 85–86

Sampson, J., 144

Sanctions, linking diversity management to, 217

Self-confidence, hypervigilance and, 151

Self-development: for black leaders, 170–173; for white colleagues, 195–200

Self-knowledge, black leader, 170–171; about others' expectations, 174; political savvy and, 139, 147–148, 157, 159–160; about relationships, 159–160; seeking feedback for, 174–176

Self-knowledge, white colleague, 195–200; political savvy and, 160–163

Self-responsibilities, 59–60

Senge, P., 72

Senior executives: behavioral strategies for, 214–219; educational strategies for, 210–214; organizational strategies and guidelines for, 209–219; role of, in setting climate, 209–210

Separatism, assumptions of: defraying, 66; white awareness of, 112–113, 206

Sexual predator stereotype, 74, 77

"Shields, K.," 22, 38, 93–94, 98, 112, 122, 131

Sikes, M. P., 17

Similarity, desire for, as source of exclusion, 99–100

Similarity assumption, 15–17; race-gender issues and, 91; white colleagues' awareness-building about, 196–197. *See also* Color-blind myth

"Simpson, R.," 57–58, 188

SKILLSCOPE, 176

Slavery history, 21, 92

Slights, misperceptions of, 109–110, 160

"Smith, A.," 79

"Smith, J.," 117

Solid, responding to requests for a, 154–155

Soul in Management (America and Anderson), 22, 51

"Spring, B.," 58

"Stanley, R.," 32, 49, 58, 99, 100, 105, 114

Status in workplace, race-gender gap in, 79, 83–84, 85–86

Stepping back, 185–186

Stereotypes: of black men, 74, 77; of black women, 78–79; examining one's, 160–161; giving equal benefit of the doubt and, 71–72; of men, 76–77; race-gender issues and, 76–79, 82; of women, 77–78, 79. *See also* Assumptions; Labeling and judging; Misperceptions; Racism

"Stewart, M.," 32, 80, 119

About the Center for Creative Leadership

The Center for Creative Leadership has a long-standing interest in the experience of black leaders. This work is conducted by the Leadership in the Context of Difference group, one of five practice areas at CCL. The overall work of this group is to develop individuals' capacities to lead when these leaders and those they lead embody values, cultures, demographics, or social identities different from those of the majority. This encompasses work on the leadership issues of not only African Americans but also women and leaders from other nations and cultures. *Leading in Black and White* focuses on the unique challenges facing black managers, providing objective and practical information about six areas of difference these leaders confront in their daily work lives.

In the area of African American leadership, CCL offers the following publications and open-enrollment program and conducts the following projects.

Publications (available at www.ccl.org/publications)

Books

Diversity in Work Teams: Research Paradigms for a Changing Workplace, by Susan E. Jackson and Marian N. Ruderman (Eds.).

Lessons of a Diverse Workforce: A Report on Research and Findings, by Christina A. Douglas (available in late 2002).

Making Diversity Happen: Controversies and Solutions, by Ann M. Morrison, Marian N. Ruderman, and Martha W. Hughes-James.

The New Leaders: Guidelines on Leadership Diversity in America, by Ann M. Morrison.

Articles

"Informal Networking and the African American Manager," by Ancella B. Livers and Stéphane Brutus, *Leadership in Action*, 20(1), 2000.

"Leading Together: An African American Perspective," by Ancella B. Livers, *Leadership in Action*, 19(2), 1999.

"Leveraging Diversity: It Takes a System," by Pamela L. Shipp and Carl J. Davison, *Leadership in Action*, 20(6), 2001.

"Single-Gender and Single-Race Leadership Development Programs: Concerns and Benefits," by Patricia J. Ohlott and Martha W. Hughes-James, *Leadership in Action*, 17(4), 1997.

Open-Enrollment Program (call 336-545-2810 or visit www.ccl.org/programs for more information)

The African-American Leadership Program (ALP) assists black leaders to explore their specific leadership development issues. Information derived from this program and its participants was one source for *Leading in Black and White*. The program encourages a frank discussion of concerns, developmental needs, and career strategies with peers who have had similar experiences. During the program, participants develop their own strategies for personal and professional growth.

Lessons for a Diverse Workforce Project

This project studied a diverse group of CCL program participants in the mid-1990s. The survey sample consisted of 160 whites (121 males and 39 females) and 128 African Americans (81 males and 47 females). The study's purpose was to explore the self-reported managerial experiences of a diverse group of individuals in order to better understand, first, the experiences that managers see as key to their own leadership development and, second, the lessons they have learned from these experiences. The study also compared the differences between African American managers' and white managers' experiences and between women's and men's experiences, as well as the differences between the experiences of men and women in the respective racial groupings.

New knowledge obtained from this study has informed *Leading in Black and White*. Detailed information about this research, including participant demographics and the specific managerial experiences identified by African American and white men and women, is available in the CCL report *Lessons of a Diverse Workforce: A Report on Research and Findings,* by Christina A. Douglas (visit www.ccl.org/publications; available in late 2002).

Further Research on Leadership in the Context of Difference

The multiyear project *Leadership Across Differences: Reconciling Ethnicity, Religion, Gender, and Culture* is designed to develop tools, techniques, and interventions that will enable practicing managers to more effectively lead groups of people with very different histories, perspectives, values, and cultures. This project is necessitated by the worldwide shift in workforce demographics, caused by such factors as globalization, increased immigration, the recruitment of guest workers, and the rising influence of minority and previously disenfranchised populations—factors that place unprecedented leadership demands on organizations' members, practices, and productivity. This project is the first attempt in the field to integrate the various complex relationships among leadership, social differences, and organizational effectiveness. For more information about this project, download *Leadership Across Differences* in the Research section of the CCL Web site (www.ccl.org) or contact project manager Maxine Dalton (Dalton@leaders.ccl.org) or Marian Ruderman (Ruderman@leaders.ccl.org).